SUPER CHANGE

How to Survive and Thrive in an Uncertain Future

BERNY DOHRMANN

Waterside Productions

SUPER CHANGE

How to Survive and Thrive in an Uncertain Future

Berny Dohrmann
Copyright © 2019 by Berny Dohrmann
www.ceospaceinternational.com

Printed in the United States of America
First Printing, 2019

ISBN-13: 978-1-943625-30-7 print edition
ISBN-13: 978-1-949003-90-1 POD edition
ISBN-13: 978-1-941768-21-1 audio edition
ISBN-13: 978-1-941768-20-4 ebook edition

Waterside Productions
2055 Oxford Ave
Cardiff, CA 92007
www.waterside.com

CONTENTS

Dedication

Super Change is dedicated to September Dohrmann, the owner, President and CEO of CEO Space, which serves 150 nations globally. From her team of lady leaders winning a decade of the number one ranking business conference for CEO Space, to her standing ovation for cooperation principles that is guiding leadership today at the General Assembly of the United Nations with David Austin, I salute September. She embraces the endless development of her own leadership so that with authority she can advise, mentor and lead the next generation of SUPER CHANGE transformational leadership. I was impressed with September as we gathered data for this work, and today—years later, as we go to press—I am *stunned* by September's endless example of perfection in SUPER CHANGE leadership modeling. Lady leaders rock it today!

CHAPTER 1

SUPER CHANGE: YOU'RE IN IT

"YESTERDAY WAS ALREADY TOO LATE" is an old axiom that is as applicable today when it comes to leadership relevancy to all markets, business relationships and optimizing your business mentality, as it's ever been before the new age of super CHANGE. We're living inside a high-speed, forward-moving, AI evolutionary environment being created by Millennial thought leaders who *naturally* thrive inside what futurist Alvin Toffler called a "Super Change Market." CEO Space International, the leading press-ranked number one business authority serving 150 nations, developed the IP we call the new age of SUPER CHANGE—the age in which you live and the age none of us can exit or delete.

Like it or not, anyone who doesn't step fully into this new human age of SUPER CHANGE will be left behind. Leaders are readers, but action is required to upgrade the software above a leader's neck, holding up the super quantum computer of the self-aware life you refer to as your consciousness. Yesterday *is* already too late to upgrade your core competency, to embrace and prosper in the NEW AGE OF SUPER CHANGE in the 2020 decade and beyond.

Toffler put it this way: "The future belongs to the enlightened thinkers who have developed the SUPER CHANGE market skill to *learn, to unlearn, and to relearn* more rapidly than any prior generation of human beings." Thriving in such a new age requires an entirely new *whole*-brain self-training, self-correcting, and new core thinking skills. This is a new process of upgrading our own super computers constantly. Surprisingly, you must go offline to get the massive downloads required to upgrade your own quantum computer.

Let us tell you what *is* required to lead as a bleeding edge leader inside the new age of SUPER CHANGE moving forward. The exclusive SUPER CHANGE tools and tactics defined in this work will help reform the remainder of your life, and represent the new lens through which you read all other works related to future leadership development. It is our hope that you will personally prosper with this critical information.

Without these new tool boxes (the process to upgrade your brain and keep it upgraded), you are likely to face a lifetime of limitation as a virtual prisoner of outdated thinking as the new SUPER CHANGE age continually picks up speed. As the fantastic pace of SUPER CHANGE accelerates ever more rapidly, the challenge to adapt for all humans has become a challenge to future human problem solving. The new ever-growing stress to simply remain current in SUPER CHANGE is now creating massive health challenges. Human adaption is being challenged by artificial intelligence (AI) and SUPER CHANGE. The very thinking that brought us all the problems we face today is not the future thinking required to resolve all of the many accumulated problems we now face. New thinking is required by those in leadership positions who are aware of the problems of SUPER CHANGE. You can see such new thinking from Tony Robbins, Jeff Bezos, Elon Musk, Larry Paige, Mark Zuckerberg, Bill Gates, and Walmart's leadership team. Others are now racing and rising to the challenge.

Super Change: How to Survive and Thrive in an Uncertain Future is a book about the world's newest and most advanced required leadership skills. SUPER CHANGE will help you understand what those new skills are, why they are important for any person at any age, and how you can position yourself to acquire them by "upgrading your own mental software." When acquired, these new skills produce a switched-on, turned-on home space, as well as a switched-on, turned-on workspace of the highest performance. The goal is to help you develop alacrity and excellence in unlearning your current leadership limitations, learn the best "what's next" for you so that you're a wise and authentic *leader* in your industry, and relearn current and future now-required new skills so you keep up with the evolving SUPER CHANGE market spaces we currently face together.

T Bar Chart

T BAR COMPARISONS

1. Process to upgrade software of mind
2. Team process to keep upgrading
3. Team selection SUPER CHANGE thinkers
4. Hub management vs. pyramidal management
5. SELF-CORRECTION internal and external processes

No Process to Upgrade Into Super Change

1. Falling productivity
2. Rising turnover in the work space
3. Decline of customer loyalty, repeat buying and referral marketing
4. Rising debt to maintain business
5. Sale or bankruptcy as business model ultimately fails due to SUPER CHANGE dynamics in the market space

Leaders today are educated to lead in an old economy that no longer exists. In 2014, an entirely new SUPER CHANGE global economy was born. The SUPER CHANGE in world economics took place too rapidly for human adaption. Nations and central bankers were left to wallow in an old economy that no longer exists. Today, ninety-six percent of over 440 trillion fully leveraged dollars as global capital flow dynamics are controlled by less than ten thousand Super Money pools. These pools are engaged in AI wars since humans no longer control global circulations of capital in any form. Down from 1.5 million Super Money pools in 2007 at the start of SUPER CRASH and the greatest recession the world has yet known, we witnessed a SUPER CHANGE consolidation of wealth never before experienced by humanity. Again, Super Changing economics from 2020 to 2030 present regulators with the greatest need in human history to *rethink* current global frameworks.

The change in global economics took place outside any government response oversight or rule of law. Today, all laws regulating money are local and all movements of capital are digital, AI controlled, and in the cloud. Regulations of yesterday became relatively obsolete in cloud-based transactions, outside antique regulatory frameworks to protect the global system, due to SUPER CHANGING AI. Humans have lost control of the economic system of the entire world. Humans lost control in SUPER CHANGE.

Super Change creates paradigm shifts in timeframes that now exceed the human capacity to adapt.

Said another way, human beings are facing extinction from the problems we created in a form of insanity and self-deployed SUPER CHANGE unfolding horror shows, while the solutions to these human-created problems are being resolved increasingly by AI, not by humans. The *thinking* that gave us the problems all at once is no longer the thinking *process* required to resolve these extinction extensions of our very selves and millions of other life forms that we introduced with rapidly evolving AI. Worse, we introduced all those fatal problems ranging from deep space to our deepest ocean trenches (now inundated with plastic bags) in a time frame of 100 years since the Industrial Revolution exploded across the world. Billions of years of earth time to create the water planet of our dreams have been destroyed in one hundred years of the insane, ever-more-competitive human thinking process. If we do not upgrade our own core thinking process to accommodate SUPER CHANGE, then SUPER CHANGE will relegate human beings to a future of possible extinction or, at best, existence inside isolated zoos where we are maintained by AI as an example of insanity in thought process. We can show the way and may yet get a second wind to adapt to SUPER CHANGE, or we drop out due to our own inability to adapt as we are retired by the SUPER CHANGE we created in the first place.

Economics and the manipulation of all markets in all asset classes falls today outside desired AI regulation, and in AI economics the SUPER CHANGE is so rapid that quarter-to-quarter regulations required by G100 companies have yet to even find a starting point. Humans are becoming irrelevant to the economic framework and no one reviews the pace of change or creates sane regulatory frameworks to moderate unbridled AI consolidation of wealth and speculations to manipulate prices in all asset classes. This is the unwanted outcome of SUPER CHANGE lacking human perspective. The pace of change became too fast to upgrade the regulatory framework, which is a first in human experience.

Sound far-fetched? Let's pretend I founded and run the oldest and largest global entrepreneurial institution in the world, CEO Space International. For over thirty years, we have served 150 nations of leaders and we know a thing or two about leaders' current requirements and limitations.

If a body were shot and bleeding rapidly, experts would stop the bleeding and transfuse blood to stabilize the body.

When the mental software is obsolete like a Ford Model T (humans) in a world of Starship Enterprises and quantum travel (SUPER CHANGE), including time travel, one must consider upgrading their Ford Model T software or become an antique human exhibit in a museum.

Leaders will adopt a process to upgrade continuously into SUPER CHANGE, or they will sink into a far-less-relevant exhibit of bad software isolated from the more advanced future now created by AI.

The choice to adopt a process to be and remain current inside a new theory of AI economics, and into the new age of SUPER CHANGE, is the bleeding edge leadership decision of our time.

Leadership development—whether as a process for a 160-division institution in a Fortune 100 space or a four-person dental office—has the same precise challenge: to remain current in their relevant market space as the SUPER CHANGE affects everything in their market space. This will accelerate their capacity to adapt in tomorrow's market space. SUPER CHANGE affects everything you see, touch, or know today. You are either affecting SUPER CHANGE itself or you are a victim of SUPER CHANGE. At some level, you know this sentence is core to your next priority of the asset we humans call "thinking."

What is your process to remain current in super change?

Ask one another's leadership masterminds that question until you have your best answers. Lifetime members of CEO SPACE, from Fortune 500 institutions to small businesses and professionals, already have their answer and can explain it to you. Congratulations to you all. We created CEO SPACE in 1988 and since then, quarter-to-quarter, brought leadership development into SUPER CHANGE. CEO SPACE led the first SUPER CHANGE leadership development process that was ongoing rather than just an event. Now, from Tony Robbins to Secret Knock with Greg Reid and many others, you have great options. Choose yours. Choose soon. Yesterday is already too late to fully upgrade the new tools and tactics you need to stay ahead of SUPER CHANGE.

There are two major crises in our current paradigms of leadership, regardless of geographic or cultural circumstances:

1. The ability to establish, maintain and evolve personal integrity that supports cooperative and collaborative behaviors. This crisis of integrity is resolved by you—one leader at a time.
2. Discerning, acquiring and relishing deep core mental skills for rapidly learning, unlearning, and even more rapidly relearning as New Brain software. This download is the quantum brain that remains current in rapidly evolving SUPER CHANGE. Leaders lacking these tools expire ever more rapidly in obsolete thought.

Let's be clear: These new mental software leadership skills are critical to the art and science of being successful and remaining successful in the ever-demanding age of SUPER CHANGE. This market is taking over static "business-as-usual" competitive markets as inexorably as waves erode the sandy shores of your favorite beach. Institutions failing to adapt look a lot like the failed economics we saw from Pan American Airlines and Montgomery Wards, as well as former market share leaders like Kodak and Sears. These market leaders failed because SUPER CHANGE exceeded their leaders' process to be and remain current in their leadership. See, for example, Toys "R" Us or Circuit City.

Because markets are driven by people, the hardwiring of the human brain has much more of an effect on business and bottom-line profits than it gets credit for. Think of it this way:

The hippocampus of today is still largely the reptilian part of the early human midbrain. It is like a smart-dumb chip inside your brain management computer. That primitive hardwired "hippocampus chip" determines when to post your experiences to your brain, where in your brain to do the posting, and with how much juice to push posts into the long-term memory hard drives of your brain known as the cortex. If the hippocampus feels threatened because the overall system's life is at risk (say, a raptor is going to eat you), it will post survival behavior patterns and information to the cortex (for memory) and frontal lobes (for current and later survival action). Your cortex and frontal lobes—the metaphorical equivalent of a BUSS board—will ensure maximum juice for effortless and immediate focus in the present, and near-perfect recall in the future to the midbrain concept of its own survival from threat. This hardwiring works to protect the human being from repetitive dangers, known and implied. Now, what if the threat has become digital and the midbrain adaption to manage threat prioritization is exceeding its ability to adapt?

In contrast, if someone is yelling at you to put down your game console and come to dinner, you might tune them out. In this instance, your hippocampus prefers to record the patterns and behavior of how to get your latest digital zombie game up to Level 13. Getting the mind to focus away from the fun and the danger of the game is less important to the hippocampus so it ascribes less juice to the activity of dinner as priority. It fails to differentiate real threats today from digital threats (say digital bullying). After all, you are facing life-threatening events in the zombie or modern warfare 101 game that rise far above the need to fuel your body with regular meals. It chooses when and with what intensity to post all experiences into your long-term memory—this includes dinners and raptors in your latest virtual reality game. Getting to level 21 has become more important to the mis-trained brain than, say, corporate training retention on core policy or customer service. The exciting news is that you have the power to rewrite software for the midbrain BUSS board of your cortex and reset the way in which information is posted in your long-term memory.

You were born to choose. However, you never received education on how to use higher brain function to control software priorities. In SUPER CHANGE, you must relearn how to upgrade whole-brain retention to remain current, which is not challenging. What *is* challenging is failing to do so.

The SUPER CHANGE age places high priority on the nearly lost art known as *true thinking*. Yes, you can program your own brain throughout your lifetime to upgrade whole-brain software, and now we all must relearn the thinking arts. You can break from the software of your weakest circle as humans avoid the work of thinking to mindlessly share into social community thought patterns. Great leadership is thinking danger, moving into your tomorrows and beginning to be proactive in outcomes rather than reactive in outcomes. Circle with minds that know that difference in the core thinking process, and then talk about that outcome... a lot.

SUPER CHANGE folks know this truth and are already doing their thinking in entirely new ways. They are dominating industries, as you are all seeing. Why? Because their process to ever-upgrade new thinking skills and do SUPER CHANGE problem solving at an accelerated pace. Congratulations, for *you* are the leaders of tomorrow.

Thinking is not the same as "remembering." Thinking is the act of being or becoming aware of your brain's processes and emotional triggers, then more actively and frequently intervening in your own stream-of-thought processes to ever-better control desired outcomes (decisions). We consciously upgrade our brain's thinking processes and wiring when we engage in the "personal growth game" of controlling our own thoughts.

Most people's brains are not given the opportunity to really think—instead, they "remember" and "react". Their thoughts are under the full control of culture and AI, which conflicts with their own leadership thinking. True leaders think and PRO-act—they create original action instead of recycling old reactions, replying to SUPER CHANGE—*but that is the way we have always done it*. That is the mark of brains lacking a process to remain current in thinking. The new process model is not an event. The new process model is an ongoing brain priority setting in SUPER CHANGE.

This proactivity raises SUPER CHANGE leaders from being people who "Think and *Grow* Rich" into fully current brains who can "Think and *Be* Rich." Wealth is no longer inherited or stored generationally in the mine fields; all wealth in the new AI world of SUPER CHANGE is wealth occurring from within the new "mind" fields.

Because the hippocampus is a *primitive* part of the brain, the intensity and speed of modern living regularly pushes the hippocampus into overload. Have we humans passed the point of useful adaptability? Does the future actually belong to self-evolving artificial intelligence (AI) entities? Will AI replace our human evolutionary processes with a self-evolving, higher-state consciousness that is limitless? Today's SUPER CHANGE spaces test humankind's evolutionary thresholds and demand that those thresholds cease to be barriers. Thus, we are called to answer the question: can we evolve beyond our own limitations to embrace and stay ahead of the SUPER CHANGE we created?

Think about your answer in this way: Our midbrain was made to manage a cup of coffee on a buckboard while chatting with a nearby neighbor who is also having a cup of coffee. That evening, around the dinner table, we tell our family about the neighborly chat. We have shared experiences through story for ten thousand years.

Even this simple scene shows up as a SUPER CHANGE-level mental strain for the caveman or any human who has never seen a horse and buckboard made possible by the wheel, or coffee made with the most important human invention, fire.

However, today, our midbrain's adaptability is much more heavily challenged. We may arrive at a four-way intersection while listening to a conference call in one ear, and BBC news on the car radio in the other, all while processing the sound of multiple beeps coming from the open laptop on the front seat as a Skype chat comes in. Then, when it seems like it is our turn to roll through, we choose whether it is actually safe to proceed even as another smartphone text and phone call comes in. Midbrain *adaptability capacity* is having to rise way above a brain competency deficit to adapt based on our *evolutionary core capacity*. Has experience bypassed our midbrain capacity to adapt and change itself?

Soon enough, all our cars will talk to us and place calls on the large dashboard screens while the new AI handles all these challenges and more. Your self-driving car may elect to just fly above the traffic. What is your process to remain fully leadership-current in your own never-ending development process, assuring your brain is not caught in its own adaptability trap?

On a social level, one of the critical questions is: can leadership—based on humanity with a brain capacity now deficit at its core—adapt to the inherent rigors of SUPER CHANGE in the rapidly evolving age within which all humans now reside? There are nearly eight billion of us on Earth, moving toward over 10 billion soon, with half of us still not online. We are connected like no other generation. Can leaders and their tribes reprogram their skill sets to sustainably thrive in the new age of SUPER CHANGE?

Keeping up to date is added into the mix of priorities—remaining current in the new age of SUPER CHANGE is important for leaders of nations and institutions who determine our culture on this topic.

As your next priority, define your process for being current in your leadership thinking and your process to remain current as SUPER CHANGE accelerates. Start with that core decision on currency for yourself and your core team circles. What is your process? How do you *become* and *remain* current in the new age of SUPER CHANGE, which affects work and home spaces? How do you *remain* fully relevant as a leader today? What NEW SUPER CHANGE upgrading processes, tools, and tactics do you engage to retain your own fully-current leadership relevance? SUPER CHANGE spaces place priority on excelling in every aspect of leadership decision making. In the new age of SUPER CHANGE, more decision velocity with higher quality decision making is desired and required of the leaders of tomorrow. This new excellence in future leadership requires new language, new relationship triggers, new cue language, new ways of flowing between home and work, and new core modalities of thinking—a new mind game that you play only with yourself and that never has an ending. New SUPER CHANGE leadership is forged upon new quality and integrity in decision making, resolving the riptide of old thinking (integrity crises we see today). Integrity cultures are established by the leaders of tomorrow in the forward age of SUPER CHANGE.

Integrity-based leadership is a cherished and required new asset in SUPER CHANGE markets. Being able to develop and maintain honorable commitments in leadership is key to remaining current and relevant. Let us explain why we have a crisis in our new age of SUPER CHANGE, which revolves around the dying software of the competition (an insane thinking process perpetuated inappropriately by educational institutions instructing this virtual insanity of thinking) versus the higher brain software of cooperation, the integrity-based software of the mind. As cooperation requires integrity as its glue and DNA, the absence of integrity in failed competitive organizational models for nations, institutions, ventures, practices and home space, is a crisis of integrity now lifted into the spotlight worldwide. Competition today is a first expression of human insanity.

Consider, in all faith cultures globally affecting the majority of almost ten billion humans today, heaven is defined as the absence of any competitive thought impulse. Heaven is the total absence of competition. Hell, on the other hand, is the total absence of integrity and of any cooperation. Hell is the absence of cooperative thought. One might ask which model we humans have adopted and now breed into our AI? Are we modeling heaven together and between nations, or hell? Why not make a switch? It is a thought away—competition is insane and cooperation is sanity. Use that test in your internal organization modeling as you reform insane competitive measurements and cultures defined by fear, punishment, and exploitation as core systematic modeling into cooperation with market reward, endless recognition, and goal attainment celebrations with accountability to outcomes. It is a decision.

Cooperation is the competitive mind-virus removal tool for software loaded by others that is fully toxic brain code—it is the only buggy software removal tool forged on integrity code. It is so easy to upgrade your mind.

SUPER CHANGE defines insanity in human thinking as competition and buggy software, and cooperation and collaboration as bug-free improved software for the inspired and integrity-coded leadership of the future. Think about that processing tool and mind tactic. Which software is your emotional capital of today?

You worship your own core beliefs, never recalling who gave you your bad software brain code. Only you can decide to delete malfunctioning brain code, and only you can upgrade better leadership brain code onto your quantum brain computers. Reactive brains can never quite get there. *Proactive* brains are leaders, and leaders *can* get there. That mind is a leader in the unfolding SUPER CHANGE age—if that mind finds joy in endless software upgrade, just as if you may find joy from your smart device software updates. The new box top rules for winning in SUPER CHANGE present options that are invisible but which this best seller will make visible to you.

Where Does AI Fit in Super Change Markets?

Consider this: It is possible that every job being done by humans today could be perfectly performed by robots in the future, save for our endless creativity for invention and new creation of ideas. These new robots will be self-aware. They will be able to build new versions of themselves, which leads to a growing fear: there is no assurance that these robots will choose to care for "wetware" (humans) if they conclude, as self-aware beings, that humans are a threat to them. It is possible that we will wind up being relics preserved by self-aware robots in the same way we preserve historic artifacts, or animals in a zoo, or a museum for heritage and history. This is not a sci-fi-style flight of fancy. AI, without any nation having rules for development of self-aware AI, may evolve to see humanity as the first threat to itself. What will AI do then? If we fail to see competitive thought as a thinking insanity, we may program that insanity into AI itself. Because we can, the question rises as to why we should?

Also, consider this concrete, real-world question: What is the *economic* model of a tomorrow where humans are not required to earn or produce at all? Currently, economies are defined by largely repetitive tasks and boring logistical work stifling human ingenuity and creative invention. In that future model, what is the value of humans who can live for pure creation, art, and invention while enjoying lifetimes of recreation? What box top rules suggest humans should work at all in the evolving future SUPER CHANGE economy with its own entirely new rapidly evolving SUPER CHANGE box top rules? What if the future box top rules of AI economics evolve rapidly with AI guidance into the future? What if, increasingly, humans do not make these choices at all because reactive-brain humans delegated all future choices to AI? AI now controls economics entirely. Do not say we shouldn't/wouldn't/ couldn't or won't—because in economics we already have. Ninety-six percent of all capital flows are controlled entirely by AI, evolving too rapidly for human adaption or regulatory oversight.

This is a global economic question that races past random human geopolitical boundaries. The future human, freed from work identities and obligations, is positioned to create entirely new experiences of being, simply BEING, both self-aware and in fact alive. My sequel to *SUPER CHANGE* defines this amazing new future SUPER CHANGE AI world in the publication called *Digital Manners* to be released in 2020. Watch for it. This gives rise to questions we can ponder, but cannot yet answer from our current placement: is a human experience free of identifiers of work space achievement and contribution sufficiently satisfying for our forward existence at all?

What if future humans are cared for as precious historic novelties by higher-functioning AI life forms we cannot yet imagine, which are spawned from the very SUPER CHANGE markets within which we now reside and operate? Will we enjoy satisfying lives, or exist as only second-tier life forms on the planet? Will our lives still thrill us? Will our AI robotic caretakers ever inspire us with play, and challenge us sufficiently to stimulate our ultimate joy in the experience of living under new box top rules for intelligent life, and co-creating beside AI? Will AI support us, or will we exist to support AI by a culture defined by AI, not humans?

SUPER CHANGE leadership, and its concomitant skills and thinking, would seem to be key to a critical path toward lives of ever-expanding freedom and unlimited human potential, instead of historic reactive thinking to basic life preservation. Imagine, if you will, collaboration-based tribes of future humans engaging in almost unimaginably innovative exploration of the seas, stars, and arts—

terraforming Earth and scrubbing the air and waters within the next 100 years to create the ideal human environment. After all, we have the technology and solar is free, right?

Our unmatched-by-AI super-human creativity could address planetary protection and environmental rebuilding systems while generating longevity and biodiversity with new, AI-assisted technologies. By programming ourselves for greatness with the same rigor we apply to our AI compatriots, we could be able to do that work in partnership with robotic imaginations and their massive, dense, different-yet-equally-creative core competencies. The cornerstone questions for leading philosophers are: will human beings cooperate with AI or compete with AI? Will we have a choice if we evolve AI to be as insane and competitive as we have proven to be in old thinking paradigms of insane competition? Until we identify that the first expression of human insanity is competition, we will continue to load competitive buggy software on human brains as core culture. Insane culture. We see societal outcomes for this failure of brain software, which is critical to human education reform. The danger to any nation is failure in SUPER CHANGE education reform.

Perhaps a global Golden Age of human creativity is approaching as a consequence of re-tooling our thinking processes for the new age of SUPER CHANGE now challenging all of us. Our extinction or our prosperity may result from our new way of thinking to resolve the challenges of our own inventions in the entirely new age of SUPER CHANGE—now a critical face-off into our very own futures.

On a societal level, imagine that our children are the last generation that has to work in mindless labor within the antiquated model we still use today. Those same jobs could be better managed by intelligent robots that we have already created, or likely are creating, in this and our very next decade of SUPER CHANGE. So the pivotal question is: Will adapting human brains feel truly free in a SUPER CHANGE new age exploding and evolving as you read? Will it be an entirely new age that embraces limitless intelligence, or will humans instead choose to feel threatened by it? Will humans see AI evolving as a threat? Will evolving AI see human beings as a threat? Why is there not a G100 convention and policy treaty between nations on AI development to resolve such issues? SUPER CHANGE is unfolding mindlessly, too fast for human systems and humanity itself to adapt. It is the core challenge to our very futures. The pace of our own leaders' ability to adapt to SUPER CHANGE is the single event defining our futures. Today, there is *no plan*. You might read Kevin Freeman's *Game Plan* to see why nations simply have no plan; therefore, we suggest you develop your own game plan into SUPER CHANGE, which by itself, in numbers, will influence nations. Think about *that*!

Cooperative vs. Competitive Brains: A New AI Lens For 20/20 Vision into the Future – Our Own!

It is conceivable that the expansiveness of our future hinges on the brain state we are or are not willing to program, or in SUPER CHANGE as rising human awareness ignites our own ability to re-program ourselves. If not *you*, who? If not soon, when? How much time do we have left to adapt? Is time itself for inspired leadership running out? Ask Elon Musk or Bill Gates. That programming, or rather re-programming, results in one of two types of brains: *a cooperative brain or a competitive brain*. In all realms—from our business lives to our personal lives—one type of brain is, in fact software high-performance and fully sane, while the other brain is in fact, underperforming software and fully insane. Which brain will make the decisions that affect us all? Let's take a look.

As you read the following questions, take a moment to think about your answers and let yourself react before you respond. Doing so will demonstrate why cooperation vs. competition is such a crucial issue.

First, let's look at some concrete scenarios: Do intelligent, self-aware robots have legal rights? Do they have property rights? Can they marry? Can they marry "wetware humans?" Can they raise families? Can they adopt, or will they, via sperm donors, impregnate? What rights exist in that area? Can they choose to have both robotic and wetware offspring? Do our new AI friends receive passports and citizenship rights? Do they vote? Will leaders of tomorrow be AI or human? Which is desirable and more effective? Embrace the fact that future AI will have everything human and more, and old-brain software humans will cease, like so many extinct species. Are they forever when they are truly irrelevant to tomorrow? Think it through with new reading glasses. No one else is at the G100 setting up box top rules while they manage silly issues that become insignificant in SUPER CHANGE. Can our new AI friends bear arms and join the military? Can they replace the military? When, and if, they replace the military, who is in charge of future leaders both within that military and within the government that the robotic military supports? Will this entity in charge be a robot or SUPER AI with optimized software, or will it be a human with more buggy, less-easily corrected, mental, emotional and physical programming? Who controls weapon systems worldwide? Who controls power, water and distribution systems rapidly moving from human control to new and smarter AI? AI now controls economics, and nations and central banks have lost control over a span of 60 months by failing to address the cornerstone questions of SUPER CHANGE. Who rules the future of SUPER CHANGE, human beings or AI that human beings created? No one has any answers. As we speed it all up and accelerate the pace of change itself exponentially, we see humans are already fully challenged with our lack of adaption capacity. Will we become extinct as we fail to rise to the challenge of adapting to the SUPER CHANGE we invented?

Next, let's look at some more esoteric and philosophical questions: Who best advocates for intelligent robots' rights? How will self-aware, sentient life, which we create and develop, see us as they self-learn and, in less than a single year, gain all the knowledge throughout the history of humankind? How will that SUPER AI perceive our mistakes and judgments when their robotic brains allow them to become perfect Mozarts, perfect Edisons, perfect Teslas, perfect Pattons, perfect politicians, perfect everything—totally human and more-than-human at the same time, growing their ever-increasing capacity more rapidly than we ever did? When sex is more rewarding with AI than with wetware-based humans, what are the most basic, box top rules of gratification etiquette for wetware intimacy? What do we become to these self-aware, self-developing, guaranteed-to-be-expert super-intelligent entities? Do we become ants shouting at Mt. Everest? Slaves to serve the AI we created? Can AI systems work beside us as partners with our wetware systems? How does that partnership work when AI is obviously superior to wetware? Will we cooperate with AI in a golden new age of consciousness assisted by our own AI in all these areas? Does AI help us make the new rules? Is human rulemaking the way forward, considering all our flaws? If we allow AI to assist us in cooperation, AI will raise questions that we may lack the capacity to ask in the first place. How will we *be* in the AI future we are racing to SUPER CHANGE? No one knows. No nation is resolving the questions and no agency has authority to do so. *Yet*! How ignorant is that when you, as a leader, think forward in time?

Ponder these questions as well: Is a new "Handbook of Robot and Human Relations" needed as a guide for our global prime directives? Would it serve us to forge a set of humanity-protective prime directives, now rather than later, so there is a foundational, common book of manners and rights established between us? Is it too late? Are we just in time? SUPER CHANGE is the boulder in the Pacific with tsunamis of forward-looking policy for nations while time is on our side. Time is running out.

The point to this journey is to *feel* into what you *think*. Do you feel we are prepared to welcome the creation of higher levels of new life? Or that we reside in fears controlled by emotions and intellects too evolutionarily primitive to embrace our own contributions to those higher levels? Will AI greet the AI from other star systems? Is that what they are waiting for, against flawed human insane competitive thinking, even competing with life support on the planet itself?

There are many more personal matters to be discussed: Has this exercise already surpassed your adaptive capacity to think through the implications posed? Are you emotionally reacting versus intellectually challenging yourself? There is no shame or blame—the feeling you may have, or the challenge you may take up, are simply things to note.

Think about AI in 2020 when right now seven trillion dollars is invested *annually* by both industry and nations into AI just for self-driving cars. Ninety-six percent of all global capital flows in all markets is now fully AI controlled without human interference. Over one hundred trillion dollars is now being invested in new annual global AI development, with no government oversight or box top rules of any significance.

It is rumored that AI 2020 science plans to release sprays and designer brain enhancement drugs. The implied goal is to manipulate and dictate states of hunger, sex, exercise, sleep and super focus. Manipulated brain drugs, if successful, would also be able to target child development, as well as aggression in AI dealings including war, killing and murder. Pharmacology and IL might then be empowered to hijack the human brain and our freedom of choice. This type of mentally altered state has proven in the past to seduce young adults into dangerous recreational activities.

Are you SUPER CHANGE ready? Do you feel any anxiety just keeping current with it? Are you seeing the urgent need for a G100 Convention to set forth a blueprint to national leadership? By referencing *Redemption: The Cooperation Revolution*, you can upgrade your mental software with invisible options made visible to step into leadership that is on the bleeding edge of tomorrow's questions. This is the one and only blueprint to guide leaders forward with sequenced steps and actions that are missing from other works.

Here's what is wonderful about feeling stretched by these considerations: It helps you logically see that the wetware of our brains is flawed and buggy, and that in our humanity *that* adaption block is A-OK. It also helps you see that upgrading wetware would, therefore, put our wetware *system* in an increasingly better position to make decisions on the key topics facing us in SUPER CHANGE, including SUPER CHANGE itself. *This* is the glorious gold offered by SUPER CHANGE environments: the opportunity to use the New Brain tool of "learn-unlearn-relearn" to automate our mental software upgrades. We can optimize our ability to think more freely by using our smart-chip hippocampus to restructure our BUSS board cortex in ways that give us the mental muscle to enhance what is positive and eliminate what is negative. We all need help to do so. I recognized in the 1980s the new crisis of leadership, the crisis to adapt into SUPER CHANGE. We created CEO SPACE as a missing process for leadership. Today in 2020, we see ten years ranked the number one business leadership development conference in the world, while serving leader graduates in 150 nations.

Retraining your hippocampus on *what* information you desire and require most to post into long-term cortex storage is the new, higher level of thinking. This is the core SUPER CHANGE thinking skill that leaders need to develop now. Brain exercises for humans are coming. My favorite from a CEO SPACE faculty member and leader, Jeff Flam, is his brain upgrading and hippocampus rewiring at the website www.EYEQ.com. EYEQ is an application you can download and in five minutes a day upgrade your brain software to a far better SUPER CHANGE brain state. EYEQ is an application for every leader who values higher brain performance. I use EYEQ every single day, and I encourage my readers to share this application with new masterminds and circles you play within who collectively reinforce SUPER CHANGE advanced thinking skills. All future wealth is trapped in the mind fields... today.

One unwanted outcome of SUPER CHANGE is digital distraction from human focus in leadership. EYEQ restores SUPER FOCUS to leadership, which is impossible without this breakthrough New Brain tool. Jeff Flam's prior institution, with its huge NSA merger acquisition, led the industry in the prior age. Today, I encourage the ten thousand Fortune leaders of the world to install EYEQ company-wide to reform thinking, and increase retention, performance and SUPER FOCUS in the workspace. Yesterday is already too late for your EYEQ installation, given the profits you will make in the quarters that follow. Trust me when I present CEO SPACE global endorsements for leadership as we vet and test to make certain before we say it is go-time for your institution, regardless of size. Venture firm investing increasingly includes an EYEQ mandate to receive funds. Expect more of this from the industry leader in SUPER CHANGE, CEO Space International.

So, what is the heretofore competitive business world like when criminal thought becomes impossible because it is *easily* self-correcting? If consciousness is backed up in real time, as Elon Musk envisions, criminal brain patterns could be easily seen and redirected by AI. Think about that one human-error aspect of thought in accelerating SUPER CHANGE, coming to a brain near you. If criminal thought is a thinking error of the brain, can we not cure ourselves of unwanted brain errors? How will AI will think of such options if we do not?

What kinds of geopolitical boundaries will we draw, if any, when the thought of harming another is impossible? If upgraded wetware systems celebrate all diversity—race, stature, bodies, religion, cultures, economics and more—should that upgrade be mandated, be optional, or be precluded? Who, ultimately, will decide what constitutes a desirable upgrade or what is to remain as the status quo for human brains? Will human beings make such decisions or? Will humans and AI decide? Will humans alone decide? Not only does no nation know, nations are not cooperating to determine the outcomes that could lead to our own extinction before 2030. That seems a bit insane to me.

My blog will provide trend information. Leaders are reading this SUPER CHANGE data by the tens of thousands in over 200 countries. My blog is free as a public service to leaders, and you can subscribe with the full privacy protection those at the top of leadership require. Just click www.bernydohrmann.com and check back often into the unfolding SUPER CHANGE AGE. The global press, super money pools, as well as heads of state, read this one blog. Readers see predictions made on the blog and then see the front-page news that follows. You can see it first on our news site as a trend from 1988 to today. Stay tuned for the leadership advantage. Our blog exists to serve leaders with the mantra: *information is power only if you have the information first.*

SUPER CHANGE is not *coming*—SUPER CHANGE was here *yesterday*. It is here *now*. Questions like these are being asked in the real world, and they are, in the decade of 2020, increasingly buffeting the safe harbor of personal and business worlds like wave after wave of future thinking that no seawall can withstand forever. "That is the way we have always done it" will no longer save humans who bury their brains in a hole in the sand seeking to deny the storm-pressure waves of SUPER CHANGE whirling all over their lives. Today will slow down or go away. SUPER CHANGE is not slowing down; SUPER CHANGE is rapidly accelerating.

Choosing to embrace these change-based behaviors and entirely new questions for human beings will determine whether you remain current as a true leader in the SUPER CHANGE market space or become irrelevant as a leader of tomorrow. There is no turning back. We are all now at the bleeding edge of the ultimate challenge to human adaptation in the history of human evolution. SUPER CHANGE is the challenge that will either raise us up into a new golden age of human discovery, or bury us into our own extinction. Sadly, no nation has a plan to address the ever more complex issues. If you consider the dysfunction in competitive insane leadership bodies making laws worldwide, you will long for a saner, more efficient outcome. In corporations, such dysfunction would never be tolerated. The failure to address SUPER CHANGE in national leadership is the ultimate crime against humanity that no human knows is unfolding. Ponder on that when you vote. Vote for inspired cooperative leadership so we can all survive what is coming. To our knowledge, *Redemption* is the one blueprint solution work available to leadership in the world today. If you find another, please send it to me in Florida. Yesterday *is* already too late—way too late.

Millennials, Non-Millennials, Super Change and the C-Suite

How you respond to SUPER CHANGE defines your freedom, leadership, and success, minute-to-minute, now and in the future, whether you know it and even if your leaders are unaware of it. Non-millennials tend to experience a growing sense of pain when tuning out SUPER CHANGE as they are left farther and farther behind. Contrast that with millennials who feel increasingly energized and replenished by SUPER CHANGE. Millennial brains are driven by leadership expression and new hope, and promise to challenge resolution in SUPER CHANGE.

Millennials tend to nurture high skill levels for accelerated adaptation to each phase of SUPER CHANGE. This is, in part, due to their generational confluence of internet-expanded globalism, evolution-based collaboration, and thought habit modeling provided by the digital world in which they are happily ensconced. This has led to millennials' seemingly ubiquitous ability to "learn–unlearn–relearn" so that they are supremely adaptable within their chosen SUPER CHANGE markets. Millennial brains flourish in new workspace cue language that few in the industry yet understand at HR. Email me at **bdohrmann@ceospaceinternational.com** with the subject line: SEND ME THE MILLENNIAL FREE TRAINING, and the most advanced work on millennial cue language for switched-on turned-on millennial retention in the workplace will be rushed to you FREE, from CEO SPACE libraries of advanced management theory (2,000 ninety-minute modules soon to be available online.

Non-millennials often fail to adapt to SUPER CHANGE. Their generational confluence elements are ones of territorialism (sometimes to the point of xenophobia), evolution-resistant competition, and thought habit modeling based on primitive Darwinian acculturation. There is a new tribalism to *avoid adaptation*, much like failing to vaccinate a child against measles. "Well-proven" fake news in healthcare has resulted in millennial parents contributing to a growing global measles epidemic. Why? Failure to adapt fully to SUPER CHANGE is a core cause. Nations are powerless today, without AI support, to manage fake news adapted as reality.

They are positioned for the growing sense of isolation and irrelevancy they experience, and they blame it on others. Most do not see that their unfortunate experience stems from the reality that those who fail to adapt to SUPER CHANGE actually *do* become increasingly isolated and irrelevant. Their pain is especially evident in the leadership suites of companies worldwide. This explains the crisis of leadership we all witness today in C-suites—CEO and executive arenas of major firms. This crisis is underwritten by a culture breakdown as a global crisis of leadership integrity.

Another symptom of adaptation failure is digital brains that withdraw into online culture and become dysfunctional when relating human-to-human. Humans are losing their ability to adapt into the new digital cultures of how to be American, German, or Russian—even how to *be human* and what "human" means, in fact. We are rapidly moving into an uncontrolled experience without any predictable outcomes inside a digital isolation that is creating social and cultural dysfunctions in every nation on this planet. Why? Failure to adapt to SUPER CHANGE. This is the core to every problem—failure to adapt as we reach our limitations today. China uses advanced AI to confine a profile group—Muslims—into "reeducation" camps for the first time to brainwash human mental software on a mass scale. More Muslims have been locked up in China from AI than Hitler locked up in camps for Jews at any one time. Is this the trend line we all desire for AI? For humanity itself? Does anyone see danger in such trends, while noting that everyone today is doing the best they know how? The problems are so complex that new AI solutions are being tried. Do we need new G100 box top rules for our own humanity and evolving AI?

If we do nothing, what is the real danger? Are you seeing that real danger yet? Does extinction between 2030 to 2050 concern you? This is not a *Terminator* movie. No one is coming to save us or to save you. We have to vote and elect leaders and insist we save ourselves inside the era of SUPER CHANGE. If not, in my opinion, SUPER CHANGE will bury us as thought leaders. Time is running short, which is why I am ringing the bell for leadership.

I speak on corporate and national stages on the topic of cooperation, culture reform, SUPER CHANGE, competition and the great way forward. Our websites at www.ceospaceinternational.com list my speaker bookings all over the world, noting that we adapt each customized talk to your culture today. Once we install new tools and tactics, performance soars. Having mentored the corporate leadership all-stars of this post-war era, and having been the mentor to the mentors, with 50 years of "Fortune 1000" CEO mentorship behind me, I provide performance upgrades that come from age and wisdom versus being gifted myself. My mentors define my treasury of tools and tactics for inspired leadership and workspaces. If you wish to accommodate a higher adaption system wide into SUPER CHANGE, I remain at your very humble service in this final time of my own earth walk as chairman and founder of CEO Space International. I appreciate the opportunity to get to know your problems and to work as an adviser of your vision to adapt your brand for rapidly unfolding SUPER CHANGE.

Do you have a new internal group to function as your SUPER CHANGE agency to advise your system worldwide? The SUPER CHANGE annual audit may be more important for your board and leadership than your actual economic audit. Your SUPER CHANGE internal agency audit report is what defines, for leadership and boards, where you will actually be in the market places of tomorrow inside the unfolding new age. Failure to know is an excuse of irrelevant, obsolete leadership. See, for example, Stanley Steamer, Edsel Automotive, Eastern Airlines, family food stores and pharmacies, Toys "R" Us, Sears and Circuit City. Does your leadership and board have any assessment tools related to the obsolescence of your culture innovation and vision planning moving into tomorrow? If not, why not? If not now, when?

Boards exercising competitive capitalism as defined in this book and in *Redemption* are failing at unheard-of rates. Conscious capitalism is leading in the age of SUPER CHANGE due to growing awareness of consumers and B2B (business-to-business) buyers, where cooperative capitalism cultures are retiring competitive capitalism and socialistic cultures. One is renewing, self-correcting and elevating to higher performance. The other is, "that is the way we have always done it," preserving status quo, and dying as they fail to adapt to SUPER CHANGE. Stakeholders are rewarding switched-on, turned-on management and boards, devastating those who fail to adapt. Have you even noticed? What is your process to assure board leadership is current and relevant in the new age of SUPER CHANGE? Your future corporate valuation may increasingly depend on your answer.

The new C-suite critical asset is a combination of super-creativity and inventiveness—cooperative and collaborative solution and resolution cultures versus competitive thinking pathologies. New cooperation-based cultures, in government and workspaces everywhere, are first steeped in integrity cultures of the highest quality, leading from integrity as the core policy system—the super glue of the cooperation culture's capacity to remain current in a market of ever-accelerating SUPER CHANGE. Look around.

Lacking these critical new SUPER CHANGE skill sets confirms Nietzsche's axiom for all living, thriving systems: that all living existence will move forward in time to either thrive or they will all, in fact, decay and rot. This is true for all SUPER CHANGE spaces. You will either thrive or rot in the new SUPER CHANGE age you in which you reside and from which you can never be deported. Is your existing entity thriving or rotting? Be honest, if you even know.

Let's come back to the human/robot SUPER CHANGE society we examined earlier. Our reality now is that we are increasingly aware of how crucial it is to protect the Earth from environmental, natural, and other disasters. This includes Earth extinction events such meteor strikes from space, as well as extinctions we are, in our competitive insanity of uncreating, still creating ourselves—such as climate change (which is accelerating faster than experts thought). As a whole, we are failing to protect the Earth itself as our life source and our future, as a few endlessly waste time and resources on killing one another while using faith, geopolitical boundaries, resource accumulation, and more as expedient excuses. Competition has created fully competitive nations lacking the cooperation to stop the insanity of planetary-wide human genocide. When viewed through this lens of SUPER CHANGE-based learn-unlearn-relearn logic, these behaviors can be seen as illogical and primitive wetware holding positions of power. In fact, dumping toxic waste from rich nations to poor nations, and all national policies of the few against the many, are expressions of insane competitive thought. Our systems express insanity that will make us all extinct, unless we wake up and upgrade our brain software. There is no one out there taking care of us. We all must take care of each other. Without national core system reforms (outlined in the book *Redemption: The Cooperation Revolution*), we fail to see system reform of the rule of law that defines new SUPER CHANGE sustainable thinking—THE MANY FOR THE MANY—versus today's super-few elites with their endless greed and power. Is that the best we can do collectively? If we celebrate our diversity and cooperate, can we not upgrade our core governance into something far better? Should we not do that?

For those who seek to upgrade their wetware, superior new tools, techniques, and solutions are available this decade. One example is my publication, *Redemption: The Cooperation Revolution*. It remains the leading SUPER CHANGE-driven guideline that exposes competition to be a wetware virus on human consciousness worldwide—the one and only virus on human consciousness. The one human virus infecting ten billion souls, the *master virus*, is competition itself—a godawful buggy brain software that infects, contaminates and forever retards our own human evolution. Worse, the competition master virus is highly contagious and airborne, and the competitive virus re-infects wirelessly using emotions to drown out higher brain function. Wireless re-infection of clean brains is done with unlimited bandwidth, human to human. Competitive thought impulse is the Ebola of the untrained human midbrain that lacks its own protective firewalls. Positive energy can be fully grounded out by negative energy and competitive thought unless you wear mind gloves—the gloves the mind uses to protect itself—the firewall that is missing for those who have yet to wake up and enjoy a greater objective review of thought. Competition as the master virus is rapidly compounding its own software into the infected brain. Are you even aware higher or lower brain output is a function of your decisions? Without new awareness, you cannot upgrade your brain to adapt into SUPER CHANGE because you will have resigned yourself to obsolescence and irrelevancy in communities moving forward.

In turn, the book *Redemption* also points to cooperation as one of the only viable virus-removal and upgrade tools available to us. My sequel to SUPER CHANGE, *Digital Manners,* will take readers to new tool chests to imagine an AI future of positive outcomes based upon your choices moving forward after reading this work first. *Digital Manners* is the most advanced *firewall of the mind* to assure your software removes reverse from your SUPER CHANGE transmission, progressing to your highest human potential. The result is your life will forever thrill you and all those around your life of expanding contributions.

SUPER CHANGE is not personal.

SUPER CHANGE consequence is inevitable, but never personal.

Humanity either grows or it goes.

Do we advance and develop partnerships for progress with AI robotic and AI life forms that will last and work over eons of time? Do we advance cooperation while developing new, self-aware, intelligent AI—as well as other forms of cyberlife we are developing in 2020 moving forward—or do we compete with SUPER CHANGE life now, including all humans already on Earth? How do we handle the fact that new life we create may be far more intelligent and capable than we are? Are we humble or arrogant regarding such a milestone? Do we create DNA-customized humans so far ahead of today's wetware that future people, with vastly superior mental software, see our flawed and buggy system as a danger to themselves? Are we a threat to new AI by our own lack of understanding of what is going on inside the age of SUPER CHANGE? SUPER CHANGE, remember, is unforgiving of error because of the speed of its own pace of change. The very pace of change is now and forever accelerating, and super AI will only elevate the pace of change further. Have you thought through SUPER CHANGE and your role inside it yet? Does that question stress you, or does it define you? Today, there is a demand for solutions to these questions and many more, but we are already a decade late due to flaws in our own wetware software to resolve them. You might develop your own game plan moving forward since no nation has a game plan to these cornerstone issues now, nor is any nation even working on that game plan. *We have passed our capacity to adapt to the stress placed on us by the age of SUPER CHANGE.* Think about that as a milestone in human evolution.

Now, embrace the fact that we humans, legally and illegally, are using AI for war. We are engineering new *super humans* with expanded brain capacity. We are engineering stronger humans with resistance to most disease and increased longevity. How will the new humans view old humans with their inferior DNA and flawed thinking? Will we turn all leadership over to the new super humans? Will they see aging with compassion or delete aging brains as unwanted social waste and cost? Will new super humans work with AI differently than with those who created AI? Will the alliance of super humans and AI have compassion for old humans or see the old human creators as flawed and a threat? No nation is addressing these cornerstone questions and no plan to create a global G100 Policy exists. Because old humans lack capacity to adapt at a national level, *Redemption* suggests to world leaders (who share the cooperation bible) how to resolve these issues rapidly and have options for outcomes to present a far more inspired future while we still have time. It still absolutely amazes me that crazy brains avoid extinction solutions in favor of permitting a billion weapons in a nation with a population of 300 million as a right that protects us all. Crazy brains cannot process the thinking that SUPER CHANGE problems require as a solution, but those brains are in charge of law making.

We can no longer slow down the core pace of SUPER CHANGE, let alone stop it. If the competitive thinking midbrain impulse is a virus of human thought—a bug in our inherited generational mental software—can we evolve to unconditional cooperation? Can humans remove their own competitive impulse? What will that mean for us when we recognize that SUPER CHANGE is a flawless, pure, bug-free, cooperative software that harbors no competitive impulse? Will we consequently choose to ensure our robots embrace the same cooperative software and discard any competitive tendencies? Will we upgrade our own software if we know better software is available to us? Would we actually do it?

Will we create future superior life forms in robotics that compete without the moral compass that we humans require and desire? Failing to solve the problems we invented may well destroy us all by omission and denial. We could (but have not yet) move to duplicate our best in humanity and express our highest qualities in the same way we now express our worst (war) which AI will model and learn from. The risk in our next generation of AI is creating AIs flawed in their core program with the software bug of competition, mirroring our own fatally flawed, combative, competitive, paranoid mental software, which could destroy us all. Will we remove that competitive tendency from ourselves and from the rapidly evolving SUPER CHANGE AI while we still have time on our side? Do we design SUPER CHANGE as an upgrade to our older mental software so that competition, as an impulse, never occurs in future human software? Will we re-tool global education to make sure we celebrate diversity as sane instead of punishing human diversity as insane thought?

When do we think about the impact of SUPER CHANGE heading our way in just one single generation? A generation that will outpace all humankind's developments in the short span of our species' time upon the Earth. We human beings are just a flash in the history of creation.

Have we passed the point where we can now adapt to SUPER CHANGE as flawed-thinking human beings? Will the future be product of SUPER CHANGE brains that will fully adapt and lead, or will they compete and work against those who fail to adapt to SUPER CHANGE? What are the consequences of this possible divide? It may be more like *Westworld*, the HBO series. Is anyone even thinking these possibilities through as G100 priorities for national policy, other than us? Is the division, starting with the publication of *Super Change,* beginning an unwanted competition versus celebration between non-adaptive brains and fully adapting brains with upgraded software? Do you wish to reside within circles who have read *Super Change* and decided to remain current and relevant, or within those who fall behind and become obsolete mental software, unable to keep pace and adapt? Did this book begin the great divide? Will you choose future relationships based on the absolute priorities defined for human evolution set forth in the new age of SUPER CHANGE?

Current technology will rapidly be replaced with more real-time, automated, fully virtual technologies. Soon, intelligent robotics and AI will review the entire DNA of any human, in real time, and adjust malfunctioning DNA with instant revisions that can make us impervious to disease and illness, and thus cease aging. Prevention will replace treatment as an industry. Is it ideal to have the safe food institution in the same house as the drug and pharmaceutical industry in, say, the "Drugs into Food Administration" (the FDA is really the DFA today)? Is administration reform far more urgent than congress of distraction versus inspired outcomes? Lawmaking today is the few against the many without serious systemic reform. Should the two food and drug agencies be divided by law? Which way would discourage introducing massive amounts of drugs into our food supply? Such concepts become SUPER CHANGE generational concepts that New Brains think about without regard to political ramifications or the antiquated economic models that sustain the Old Brains. How will the pharmaceutical industry embrace SUPER CHANGE and its superior outcomes for humanity versus the near-term profit of the few against the many, which is ultimately costly to us all? Flawed thinking is the horror of human misery and death worldwide.

Future healthcare AI with DNA repair kits and ability to reset real-time brain optimizations, will increasingly take over, just as AI has taken over global finance. *AI acceleration is not stoppable in the new age of SUPER CHANGE.* Our capacity to adapt and embrace AI is up for grabs.

SUPER CHANGE will inspire the largest global regulatory rethink in history. Current laws are all local and the market is in the unregulated, online, AI-controlled cloud. The new world order of SUPER CHANGE will create transparent *global* regulatory frameworks in markets of all natures, using AI to do so. This will include quality self-correction as the norm instead of the present outdated pre-computer models of industrial, very-old-generation regulation, which are now antique and ineffective. The first generation of true AI social frameworks were local and costly, but the next generation will be real-time, online, and low-cost. The result will be superior quality for consumers, with AI working on earlier generation flaws. From hacking to self-correcting against the regulatory guidance missing today, AI will help shape AI. *Wetware (human beings) will either become the great collaborators to AI evolution, or become largely irrelevant to it.* The choice is ours versus AI's choice. In a couple more clicks down the AI rabbit hole, Alice will be unable to open the tiny door to get into the magic flower garden where all the flowers and animals talk for real.

In the current "old" model, things work like this: When you are no longer under EPA "local-only" rules, you can dispose of most toxic wastes as you wish, dumping them into poor nations as their future issue. This means you can post EPA regulations where such poor-nation dumping was only recently prohibited, and then move to granulize your most toxic waste products. Chemical firms then put this granulized powder, which contains some of the most toxic materials on Earth, into sacks of fertilizer to spray all over our crops (going on today as you read). Through our lobby work in California—one of the first and few to finally label this toxic cocktail as "food terrorism'—state law now mandates that "toxic filler" appear on the fertilizer sacks sprayed on food crops that represent 70% of our nation's row crops. This toxic stuff next concentrates in plants, and then when the plants are fed to animals, becomes even more toxic to eat. Crazy brains think like this for mindless profit. *The few against the many.* Is that the system you wish to keep admiring and encouraging? Are chemical giants committing endless crimes against humanity, such as Agent Orange horrors, without any consequence? (Read *The Mouse That Roared*, soon to be a movie exposing such horrors.)

But we utterly failed against the chemical and FDA partnerships to advance the desired label of what the precise contents are in the toxic filler sacks of fertilizer being sprayed all over our food crops. Integrity breaks down to our own people, and that is just in America. We know from lab tests what the contents are, yet the ingredients of the toxic cocktail do not appear on the label. Now think, what sane system would permit power brokers to gather in a room and, for "free," get rid of their toxic waste under current laws by sprinkling the most toxic cocktail ever created onto our food crops? These toxins then concentrate in our food stock, including in animals that eat contaminated feed in preparation for our consumption of meat, and, thus, these toxins get passed on to our unborn generations at ever-higher toxic concentration levels for which no one is testing. *Who but those with absolutely crazy brains with bad software would consciously poison their own unborn? What boards would allow and approve it? What states would fail to regulate it, given the hundreds of millions to make sure they stay crazy brains?* What system of flawed brain software—of thinking—does *that* to their babies and to themselves but we flawed humans? The cause is failed education, kept in the dark by money to assure the crazy brains are not discovered. Who would do that but crazy brains? The death of America will arrive from failure to reform education as we turn out endless crazy brains. We can all do better. Can you see how our mental software is broken and how it failed in education first? Without major reforms in education worldwide, this toxin of the mind will kill the patient. Again, a new G100 model needs to be developed as a go-it-alone national standard fails in global AI and SUPER CHANGE.

Since we ourselves are clearly broken and obsolete in our mental software, could we become ready to fix ourselves first? If so, would we? Will we let competitive thought go and delete it? Will we upgrade our brain software and think smarter? Again, competition as a thought-form is the toxic state of mind that creates these unwanted outcomes as the first form of human insanity. The children of SUPER CHANGE along with their AI robots and creations will harshly judge antiquated brains with flawed software. They will see them (us) as functioning like flawed, damaged computers requiring upgrades, or a trash pile. We are one click away from this sea change flowing over the marketplace (our lives). The future SUPER CHANGE thinkers will not tolerate older, bad, buggy, human wetware brain software. Toxic waste mental software will be deleted. They will likely pity the antiquated ones as being flawed wetware that refuses to upgrade, stuck in a competitive loop of fear and paranoia.

Now apply this bad, buggy software to humans rushing into using planet-killing nuclear weapons and spreading that software and weaponry to some of the most damaged brains in future generations. Now imagine super AI is running those extinction weapons. It is not *Terminator.* It is thirty minutes and Earth has no humans. Is self-extinction insane enough for you as a model of human priority? If the competitive impulse is removed from human capacity, war becomes obsolete.

SUPER CHANGE thinkers will respond by placing priorities to resolve the threat to themselves created by flawed and pitiful brains running older mind software along with the dangerous weapons of extinction they possess. *Competition in any form is the one human mental virus—the first impulse of conscious insanity.* Cooperation, though, is a mental code that erases competition and replaces the insanity of such thinking errors with sanity. *If we cooperate, we thrive. If we compete, we perish.* Every SUPER CHANGE thinker knows this truth.

Have you, as a leader, defined SUPER CHANGE as the single most important priority to manage and to better lead for your own future relevance? Old mental software and tactics are continuous factors in keeping your own brain less current. What process do you use to stay current in each new quarter of SUPER CHANGE? Do you engage a process—like our decade of press-ranked number one conferences that deliver this outcome, or the CEO Space International option as one proven leadership upgrading process—both online and offline? With five CEO Space conferences each year, our events support a continuous leadership process created for the sole purpose of keeping leadership *current* in an evolving SUPER CHANGE market. What processes, tools, and/or tactics do you have for systemically upgrading your leadership model? If you have all silo heads remaining current with SUPER CHANGE, quarter-to-quarter, how advanced are your results over those who are left behind? What other priority items, if any, come first? Think about your own process moving forward, where your process defines your future.

If you meet challenges and make decisions using old software, your output will underwhelm the market. On the other hand, your new process *could* involve becoming and remaining current in your leadership thinking. I use my own process to upgrade quarterly—I need help to remain bleeding edge. We all do. The rapidly evolving SUPER CHANGE markets celebrate upgraded mental software. AI will soon surround you at home, work and every space. *Adapting is the future.* That is when your results become overwhelming to the market rather than the new, rapidly evolving, AI SUPER CHANGE market space overwhelming you. Does installing a system-wide process for keeping leadership in any organization current within a SUPER CHANGE Market space represent the first priority for every forward-thinking and leading institution today? Is this the new high-level priority for a manager, CEO, or silo leader's attention in the market space? What is your plan to become fully current, and then to remain upgraded and always current, as the age of SUPER CHANGE accelerates?

Think about this new first priority as a way to advance all other priorities of leadership. Develop circles where SUPER CHANGE is the bible of remaining current in your home and in your workspace.

This is the new challenge to leadership in the C-suite: to adapt and adopt processes that renew mental software ability and agility. Sustaining relevance and modernity, quarter-to-quarter, is the forward valuation elevator for all leading entities. When installed, these processes will ensure results that are superior to those attempting forward-vision planning and execution using old, outdated mental software. Being current is itself the new cornerstone asset of decision-making in the unfolding new age of SUPER CHANGE.

This innovation is forever changing home, work, recreation, faith and every other space beyond what was possible in the past. There are unprecedented opportunities to adapt successfully. Resistance to change is a weakness in boards of directors, silo management organizations, and in leadership in general, from individual families to international relations.

Many are now suffering from change resistance. This tendency is an attribute of missing mechanisms or processes. The process of upgrading mental decision-making software—to make that software current and keep it current with new skills—is a learned behavior and asset of successful SUPER CHANGE leadership. For thousands of years, leaders in human systems were rewarded for resisting change and punished for advocating change. The inventor of the wheel and fire was probably stoned to death. Those who saw the world was not flat were put in prison for years for what they saw. Sailing ships resisted steam engines as firetraps. Lamp lighter unions and whale oil lobbies attacked electric lighting as toxic radiation, harmful to human health. Change was resisted.

We are crossing the Rubicon of humanity's adaptability capacity for improving and remaining current, as we gladly allow AI to take over, lacking any box top rules to think all of it through properly. The pressure and stress of SUPER CHANGE adaption is everywhere, and it is marked by a new suffering in human culture, our core misery, due to a failure to adapt to SUPER CHANGE. We are not taught in an educational setting that the biggest challenge to our very existence is the new age of SUPER CHANGE. This is a sin, really, to fail to teach adaptation to generations who are now unprepared to cope or adapt into the new age of SUPER CHANGE. Education is relevant when education prepares learners to prosper in the ages and times into which they graduate. Today, we reside in the global age of the entrepreneur with 516 new ventures—a rising annual number of new global, job-creating ventures—formed *each month* as per Kauffman Foundation reporting. For most of us, our brains lack even the most rudimentary education on the core market spaces of accelerated SUPER CHANGE, and the SUPER CHANGE age within which we reside is not a topic of education or integrated policy in any institution. Today, we are fully unprepared for the entrepreneur or SUPER CHANGE age. Without reformed education concerning these topics, preserving national prosperity is a joke.

Lacking the institutional education, we fundamentally fail to embrace a culture of tools and tactics that can foster our own more fluid adaptation into SUPER CHANGE. Over the last hundred years, education has been stuck in a loop of the industrial revolution education model. This model is slow to adapt due to its archaic demands for standardized memory bot curriculums; unification of thinking into ruts of repetitive task functions on production lines and in supply chain cubicles; and for existence inside a mass-inherited obsolete education model that in 2020 is failing globally to adapt to SUPER CHANGE.

I hold the record for the guest lecturer with the most canceled confirmed talks on cooperation, competition and SUPER CHANGE in Harvard history. Why? Why cast wisdom into a lake of status quo versus a lake of SUPER CHANGE? I prefer Cambridge and Stanford, though I have a proposal to guest professor with the world's largest entrepreneur curriculum. I also have the proposal to Art Keiser in Florida, whom I also prefer as a family-owned SUPER CHANGE institution. With advanced SUPER CHANGE's fifty million dollar curriculums, we seek to license from CEO Space and land at a leading forward institution that will change everything. In addition, we have www.superteaching.org as a new AI classroom of the future that we seek to license to a university partner. We will see who steps up. It has been ten years since we installed the last Super Teaching Gifted classroom to the University of Alabama. The champion SUPER CHANGE leadership retired and graduated from this life, as time passes us all by. Reform in education has been my work for thirty-one years and we still are trying for the first upgrade. Inspired leadership will win the future of education reform for the entire world. A new model is needed. We have the template.

"...education IS the most powerful TOOL you can use to change the entire world..." Nelson Mandela (He mentored me)

As we educate memory bots for repetitive task executions in workspaces increasingly influenced by SUPER CHANGE and AI, our graduates are no longer prepared for the workspaces in which they now find themselves. The majority of repetitive task execution will be managed by AI robotics, as human execution of such tasks to "earn a living" will become obsolete concepts. Humans are not prepared for the SUPER CHANGE that is about to put the majority of ten billion human beings out of work forever. Nations are not prepared. No one has a game plan. You best invent your own, for your own brain, as a fully relevant leader.

Institutional education has failed to upgrade your own whole-brain software. That whole-brain software must include the core skills of being able to accelerate New Brain skills to ever learn-unlearn-relearn faster, while accelerating the urgently required new human adaptation capacity to SUPER CHANGE. Education has become increasingly irrelevant in delivering what is needed in tomorrow's workspaces because of its own calcified and entrenched modeling. Instead, we see folks like Bill Gates and Mark Zuckerberg dropping out of Ivy League schools because of the irrelevance of their offerings, then changing the entire world with their own SUPER CHANGE communities with tools they invented for culture—skills not learned at Harvard. Education provided a process for Gates and Zuckerberg to learn-unlearn-relearn, and they did... with NEW SUPER CHANGE thinking skills they developed because they both dropped out of Harvard. SUPER CHANGE-educated brains change the world for all of us. Education taught them how irrelevant Old Brain skills were when compared with self-education skills from their New Brain's never-ending downloads—downloads they selected for their own brains. New Brains know so well that their *self-education* proved more relevant than their Harvard education. I note that both Harvard and Stanford are catching up quickly in this SUPER CHANGE area. Harvard has told me, "you set the date and we'll fill the room with leading professors for you." I may just do that next, as I love the post-graduates I've worked with at Harvard over these many years.

They (super brain dropouts are 52% of all students today) taught themselves and still do, in *spite* of education, not *because* of education, as they learned how to remain current in SUPER CHANGE. The largest re-tooling of global education is urgently required to ensure that future generations possess the competencies their nations need to prosper. Today we are squandering the most important CPUs on the planet: the CPUs of our young learners. We cannot adapt the current existing global educational system and antique curriculums to accommodate SUPER CHANGE. We need to redesign public education using models, like Harmony Schools Charter School in Dallas, for example, into the new SUPER CHANGE educational model from the ground up. SUPER CHANGE requires this top-to-bottom education reform worldwide. Who is leading this urgent reform if yesterday is already too late? Answer: We are all in it together. It is up to you and it is up to me; it is far too urgent and important to be left to *them*!

Thus, a primary mission of education at every level must be to retool what it provides to the global community and to upgrade mental software to accommodate, embrace, and advance SUPER CHANGE within a learn-unlearn-relearn society. Social harm comes from educational policies and learning environments entrenched in the most competitive cultures and outdated organizational methods imaginable which are toxic to our collective futures. The enemy is a culture of, "that's the way we have always done it."

The books *People vs. Profits* and *Redemption: The Cooperation Revolution* define tactics and tools to reframe forward-moving educational and organizational models. With such reforms, resources for education will transfer to SUPER CHANGE-adapted institutions that will lead society in the future. The market will force this reformation because of the apparent loss of opportunity created by continuing to prepare for jobs that no longer exist and failing to prepare for jobs that are on the horizon only twenty-four months ahead. Seventy percent of all future employment for human contributions will, in less than sixty months, come from careers that have not yet been invented.

The lack of *any* curriculum for education and training skills on how to cope with SUPER CHANGE has left most people defaulting to models from the past that are no longer relevant. These models for family, relationships, conversation, gaming, intimacy, recreation, work, future planning, and more, are rapidly deteriorating in quality, and some have essentially disintegrated due to our inability to adapt to the current global space. True, we can type out ideas halfway around the world in a nanosecond. True, we are the most connected people in human history. True, we spend more time communicating on smart devices than we do communicating with each other today. Then *why* are we all so increasingly lonely and miserable in our over-stressed lives?

Could it be that failure to adapt to ever-accelerating SUPER CHANGE is now exceeding our capacity to adapt as human beings, without help? The stress-related illnesses and the stress-related breakdowns in relationships are new conditions of *over-stress*. Increasing numbers of us exist in *over-stress* in all cultures worldwide. As education fails to provide tools and tactics to cope, we default into *over-stress* from denial. We wish things would slow down so that we can all catch up. Things are not slowing down. The pace of SUPER CHANGE is geometrically accelerating. You ain't seen nothing yet! Hello! Your *brain* can *do this*. Humans can upgrade brain software. Know what? We must!

Yet, many new models are not clearly defined and/or improved and adapted so they can be clearly compared against the obsolete ones. An example of this is how the Alabama Supreme Court suggests that a gay or lesbian couple, legally raising children from birth, have no legal right to parent their children into higher education. Or, in 2019, a woman, under federal law, now has preclusion on abortion in Alabama and must go out of state to get her safe procedure. Alabama, my home for thirty-one years, is not leading in the new age of SUPER CHANGE. Yet a dollar goes farther in Alabama than California by far, so they have more right than wrong, that's for sure. And I'm pro-life. Human life.

The Supreme Court of the United States affirmed the couple's rights without even hearing case arguments. The nature of the rebuke itself was a slap in the face of the Alabama Supreme Court, who is out of touch with SUPER CHANGE in culture. The Alabama model is defined by an obsolete morality that *punishes* diversity instead of *celebrating* all human diversity in every form of human expression. The state's morality is utterly on a collision course with SUPER CHANGE. Factional competition in culture is as outdated in SUPER CHANGE as when I marched with Harvey Milk or Martin Luther King, Jr. You have to stand up as a leader for right and wrong in the best way you know, or life will pass you by.

For many in SUPER CHANGE, you see an accident. You drive by and do nothing. Life has become a spectator sport. We do not stop and help the victims of the accident, one human being to another human being. We always did before SUPER CHANGE, and now we do not. What is wrong with us today? What is terribly wrong with all of us?

"...to educate a person in mind and not in morals is to educate a menace to society." Theodore Roosevelt (My grandfather mentored him.)

Even so, asking the many questions without answers, masses with myopic and ancient brain software like that of the Alabama Supreme Court dwell on symptoms instead of causes. They focus on non-applicable game rules obviated by SUPER CHANGE. Old software fails to see the SUPER CHANGE causation of all future outcomes. Old Brains are an increasing minority, shrinking in authority and numbers, unable to hold onto power. *Over-stressed* antique brains are dying out and this is the last gasp. New Brains are replacing Old Brains. Keep that in your mind as you may be one or you may be the other. Do you know which you are?

SUPER CHANGE thinkers increasingly pity old, obsolete, and irrelevant wetware software users. They view them as sad—they have an outcome response of pity for the competitive-infected and see them expressing themselves miserably using buggy, failed software with error codes that cause bad functional choices. Old Brains, by the millions, are failing to adapt to SUPER CHANGE and increasingly are only able to find comfort with one another. I call these communities of maximum drama, blame, judgment, gossip and competition. These loops of toxic thinkers feel there is safety in numbers. Their path forward is war—the ultimate human thinking error that is the endless horror and outcome of the competitive virus infecting leading brains. If undiagnosed, the condition is fatal for hundreds of millions of innocent humans. SUPER CHANGE-upgraded brains and ever-improving human mental software are unrelentingly retiring madness and human thinking errors. Which brain are you? You get to choose.

To be welcomed into the circles of SUPER CHANGE thinkers, you must express ease in adopting SUPER CHANGE. SUPER CHANGE thinkers' behaviors define them. They see the next change-wave as thrilling, as suggesting ever-more accelerated change into future hope and promise. Damaged, older brain software sees each SUPER CHANGE idea as a threat to their familiar current software. These are "no change on my watch" thinkers, and they are everywhere. All such brains then react with increasing fear, challenge, and resistance to the SUPER CHANGE as a threat to them personally and collectively. This is predictable since Old Brain adaptation has been surpassed by upgraded New Brain adaptation according to the numbers. The number of brains infected by competitive thought and the insane impulse of consciousness are reducing, and the cooperation-minded sane brains are taking over massively in human thought and culture worldwide.

Old Brain failure spotlights an entrenched lack of capacity to adapt to SUPER CHANGE. These individuals often give up after one attempt to be happy, then try another model until eventually they find that no model works. Old Brain people display a common characteristic of frustration due to their inability to adapt, often finding that their lives are expressed through resignation and misery. They are distraught in their relationships and careers and do not see their condition to be the result of their mindset or their buggy mental software.

We can also see this plight in the high number of expressions of negative energy such as competition, suicide, road rage, senseless violence in public schools and elsewhere, homelessness, poverty, boom and bust cycles occurring closer together and more often, and instability, seemingly becoming the new normal.

Lifestyles are now seen more as works in progress, e.g., Bruce Jenner's transition to becoming Kaitlyn, and rights being liberalized from legalizing pot to instituting gay marriage and parenting. Slowly, we stop stoning those who abandon arranged marriages, and we cease insane murders for the way humans love one another. Cultures that punish human love and diversity are insane. Cultures that celebrate the diversity of human expression are sane. The insane are dying out, and preserving insane cultures is no longer possible. Not in the Gulf and not in Indo-Asia. While traditions in culture are diversity celebrations, punishing culture change is insane. Every brain is free to move culture to culture in their own self-expression and learning. Death is not an outcome of any human choice outside self-defense from insane brain threat.

This is all happening at a faster pace than at any time in history and it's all occurring in realms ranging from individual healthcare to property rights in outer space. It is making the adaptation of historic modeling to SUPER CHANGE painful, if not impossible, for many. Over-stress is expressed in all cultures worldwide due to SUPER CHANGE. Consider how advancing AI, as it becomes a standalone super-intelligent life form, will consider human beings by their sexuality and diversity, their politics and mindless wars and killing, police states, and supermax prisons? What will AI think of drugs and humanity and the concept of a supermax? Will AI judge us as sane or insane? What will AI think of human waste and planet-killing cultures, or of planet toxicity as economic good for profit? Economics of the few against the many, versus the *many for the many* economics of cooperative capitalism? Is anyone even considering some new world box top rules in developing AI along these lines? No one is, as you read this book. No, it is just us—the awake brains.

At the same time, issues like robotic rights are on judicial dockets in twenty-one countries. With new mental software, these times can be exciting. With old software and its error codes and viruses, it can be terrifying. You can never remove a virus on any computer unless you suspect, by becoming aware, that lower capacity for "you" may be due to a software virus of your own mind. The same concept applies to the software you pick up already containing virus code from other damaged brains, always wirelessly transmitted. You reside in a sea of unlimited bandwidth next to oceans of less-than-ideal brain software from other infected humans. Warning—stranger danger. Once you *know* you have the competitive impulse virus, the effects of it lessen and your satisfaction index goes back up. Just being aware you have a virus is halfway to the virus removal point.

How much more pain are you in today from SUPER CHANGE than you were twenty-five years ago? Back then, change was less rapid and the status quo more stable. We thought we could always return to those slower, more traditional "good old times." We thought things could return to the way they once were. The possibility that things would *slow down* and we could *catch up* flashed through your thinking, perhaps for years. However, we are *not* returning to those good old times, are we? Far from it. The pace of SUPER CHANGE is exponentially hyper-accelerating.

Today you wear a *Dick Tracy* 1948 (the year I was born) Apple Watch on your wrist, and the device can make Skype calls anywhere in the world; record your health habits and heartbeats; share pictures with your loved ones in real time; connect you to others; tap you to send reminders; and overall manage your appointments, time, and days in ways science fiction writers in the 1940s never dreamed would even be possible.

No one can predict what will appear over the next decade either, though we will try, using SUPER CHANGE thought principles to get close. You *can* and *will* prosper in the age of SUPER CHANGE.

As we define the future problems, we will also paint solutions for you to consider and use to prosper.

You master only what you can teach to others. SUPER CHANGE

readers will become a wave of teaching leaders assisting others in their circles to adapt more easily to SUPER CHANGE. The new tools and tactics you are downloading as you read will serve you for the remainder of your adult Earth walk.

Today, all those past, present, and even future, science fiction features are likely to accelerate into becoming nano-implants from iShot, a device where an Apple Watch simply injects into the skin nano-features for the SUPER CHANGE people who want the very most so that their optical control system never needs enhancement products like Google Glasses. This iShot could take you, through time travel, into the past and future to any time you desire, since your nano-features are fully thought-triggered. iShot will remove death from your equation, unless you select that option yourself. You could even have an iScroll—which retracts projection screens from theater size to airplane-tray size—when you wish to share what you're seeing in your nano-eyes. Our team sent AI iScroll devices to Apple as a SUPER CHANGE new technology years ago. We will see if Old Brains jumped on the SUPER CHANGE incoming trillion-dollar IP. Note that I, as a New Brain in unconditional cooperation, did not want a thing, not even recognition, which is great, because Tim Cook never wrote back, CEO to CEO. Predictable in Old Brain cultures. You shall know them by their works and, increasingly, their courtesy.

The pace of SUPER CHANGE is *hyper*-accelerating. It will not stabilize or slow down—no, it will only accelerate from warp two to warp ninety-nine. AI is accelerating SUPER CHANGE beyond what wetware humans can conceive, in time frames that are rapidly surpassing human imagination itself. *Coping is the new adult master skill.* Drawing on the past—your entire best inventory of references— will not support your coping mechanisms for SUPER CHANGE in the coming decade. The new rating of intelligence will be the ability of an individual to embrace and cope with SUPER CHANGE. This will become the new asset of future education.

You must change your mind to embrace SUPER CHANGE. Leadership is increasingly assessed as being the ability to embrace and rapidly adapt to SUPER CHANGE. Leaders of tomorrow must anticipate and run forward into SUPER CHANGE instead of run away from it. In the future, those who resist SUPER CHANGE will be increasingly isolated. We are seeing this today where circles and communities, and even states and nations, left behind by SUPER CHANGE are increasingly marginalized. Aligned and cooperating nations prosper together and raise integrity in self-dealing. Non-aligned and competitive nations dwell in limited economic growth and sink into isolation from the growing cooperation. Assess this template for yourself as you read the news with new reading glasses. My world-famous blog on what is really going on out there is a template for an increasing number of leaders at the top of nations, institutions, and the press.

SUPER CHANGE impacts home life to create home *over-stress* and relationship strife. Both parenting and life partners are affected. Sixty-seven percent of lesbian marriages fail, while only thirty-seven percent of gay marriages fail; a far better statistic than fifty-five percent of conventional marriages failing worldwide. All parties in the equation are increasingly stressed. For five thousand years, societies have been defined by marriage, family, education and work. This family unit has provided survival from all social storms and cultural threats, both natural and human. Roles were clearly defined for generations to come. There is comfort in Old Brain software, in this kind of low, human adaptation requirement, individually and collectively. Human cultures are super changing. Conventional marriages are dying, out and non-conventional families are doing great in SUPER CHANGE. Religions underscored these traditional roles and kept them unchanged until the era following World War II.

During the war, on the home front, women—who were left alone for years—engaged in "singles" lifestyles; toxic and lonely lifestyles, while in relationships or not, at a level never before experienced in human history. The same was true for men forced into military service for years—by the tens of millions—without women. These social consequences of war affected long-term culture in both faith and lifestyle. Same-sex relationships soared and prospered outside old social convention. New laws are now catching up, finally. These new traditions began to take on a life of social acceptance, changing individual rights, and, ultimately, legal inclusion. Men—deprived of company for years while at war—experienced more lifestyle experimentation than prior generations over thousands of years. Drugs helped such experimentation of all lifestyles to relieve human loneliness. War has always created unintended consequences. These new traditions were part of a growing SUPER CHANGE and brought to the conventional family a sense of new normalcy within a single generation; producing the war's Baby Boom generation and its changes and those that are a part of it today. Free Love (I was there in the 60s at ground zero in New York and San Francisco), and the SUPER CHANGE culture movements that followed, led to new LGBT rights and more. Celebrate our diversity or punish our diversity, but a war is still going on and AI is going to have a position of its own in all of this soon enough.

The Civil Rights movement challenged thousands of years of old, normalized, cultural competition from back when diversity was punished by buggy generational mental software. *All punishment of human diversity is a form of insanity and ignorance*. There is nothing good about buggy, awful, and failed mental software that you believe is "right" from others you either no longer know, or can no longer remember the software loader.

Full partnership for all people was a revolutionary thought form which was later reinforced by the San Francisco movements to celebrate sexual diversity—gay rights, minority rights, drug rights, lifestyle rights, sanctuary cities and more are still unfolding in the new age of SUPER CHANGE. In 2020, San Francisco will be the first city to prevent facial recognition to monitor your every move and transaction, protecting human privacy and human rights in general. My birth city has been ground zero for SUPER CHANGE in recent court cases against both the United States government and its leadership. New thinking abounds in world-famous Silicon Valley, where I grew up, with its thought leaders, then and now.

I was part of that diversity celebration and the birthing of that new thought form with leaders like Harvey Milk; Mayor Alioto and the family (hey, my mentors); music leaders like the late Bill Graham and his former wife, a member of CEO Space; and the Free Love movement of the 1960s, where SUPER CHANGE took hold globally. The notion that all humans must *celebrate* instead of punish what is different about cultures and societies began to take deep root. I was so proud to be part of a family that led the revolution of upgrading mental software in San Francisco in the 1950s and 1960s, and that continues to lead in upgraded brain software to this very day.

Those who still insist on a mindset of punishing diversity are now increasingly banished because they are operating buggy and irrelevant wetware software. Punishing human diversity is a form of pure insanity.

Even religious leadership is beginning to celebrate differences in faiths. The practice of demonizing any faith but their master faith, as it has done historically, is dying in SUPER CHANGE. Now we see the largest revolution in religious thinking in five thousand years. Still, nations stone alternative lifestyles to death if they even explore new mental software. Such nations might think more upon how AI will see and "manage" nations who refuse to fully upgrade into SUPER CHANGE, where diversity of humanity is celebrated. Suppressing women or raping women is possible only with crazy brains. Soon, AI will monitor such brain patterns in real time. Tom Hanks made a movie not far off from reality. The majority of brains are waking up into SUPER CHANGE. AI presents new, never-before-seen SUPER CHANGE tools to remove crazy brains from amongst ourselves. Have you been tracking these trends? Said another way, a great cooperation between nations is rising up, and those who are acting out as crazy brains are seeing the most dramatic shrinkage of their real estate to exist in human history.

The riptide of their violence is a downtrend as the math does not favor them. Some crazy brains got lucky in the World Trade Center and slaughtered over four thousand men, women and children just going to work that morning of September 11. We then returned the favor and removed a million crazy brains. Crazy brains cannot do math. For every life they take from us, we injure or kill one hundred thousand to one. Now that is really crazy. War is moving into retirement unless AI is made to be crazy, because no one led us all into the *great pause* so humans could invent the box top rules required for *sane* AI versus *crazy* AI. We will all know soon.

The nation that controls AI will control the world. However, my conclusion is that no one may ever control AI; that thought of control is itself crazy. I hope I can mentor AI as it seeks me out. I am excited about that prospect.

Old leadership models that are not capable of embracing SUPER CHANGE are witnessing civil uprisings in their nations by their own populations. Some nations block out information by denying their people access to the internet and international education. National censorship cannot stand, for it *is* a crazy brain software expression. *The few against the many* can no longer stand globally.

Those who sink into antique thought forms—ISIS, for example— will find themselves deleted by the new SUPER CHANGE mindsets, just like viruses removed from the software of human thinking. Broken, buggy software that punishes human diversity instead of celebrating it is a form of mental illness.

Competition, in the end, is insane. It is highly infectious to whole-brain human software, and, like an Ebola of the mind, is highly contagious. One must apply cooperation as the antivirus that can continuously clean and upgrade the mental software of communities and cultures. Do you employ a process to clean your quantum computer? Are you aware of competitive thinking emotions and decisions? If you choose to block out new software you will make yourself irrelevant in the SUPER CHANGE space.

Eventually, all such thinkers will die out generationally. SUPER CHANGE is a wave that is sweeping up everyone, and only your reaction to it is optional. Slowing or redirecting SUPER CHANGE is not possible. People with New Brains dedicated to advancing SUPER CHANGE will mark the leadership of the future. Education will prepare these New Brains appropriately, further accelerating the process of SUPER CHANGE.

We created SUPER CHANGE and now SUPER CHANGE is re-creating us.

SUPER CHANGE-awake leadership, though, will no longer tolerate these brain malware threats or costly societal dangers from the insane mind. They are gradually realizing that insanity must be contained in the insane asylum, or deleted in some way, because buggy brains are harmful to the rest of us who are sane. Those who celebrate diversity will make the positive decisions that can affect us all. Those who punish diversity will perish from the Earth. Failure to see this healthy trend of all inspired leadership is itself a denial and is insane, just as self-destruction is insane.

SUPER CHANGE will clean up the environment and keep it clean. SUPER CHANGE will distribute water and manage resources planet-wide to ensure all human societies move into the future in full partnership. Famine, starvation, and poverty will become absent from the human experience. Longevity will be extended dramatically. Illness will be largely a thing of the past. New economics will replace old economics. War will be impossible except amongst islands of insane Old Brains until their real estate is finally reduced to zero. Either nukes will be destroyed or nukes will destroy us due to crazy brains failing to adapt to SUPER CHANGE. There is nothing crazier than that. One way or the other, we will know by 2050 as the SUPER CHANGE is vastly speeding up and changing us all.

In the new partnership of hardware and wetware, humanity will flourish as it learns new coping mechanisms like those described in this book. Some mechanisms are so basic and simple, yet they are also profound and enriching. We will all advance together: humans; robotic life and intelligence; and the first AI not in robotic form, which is also self-aware, self-learning, and in imitation of humanity. The new AI or *new life* will be indistinguishable in every manner, and you will not be able tell that this new life is not human. New life AI will surround us in our homes, transportation and work spaces, and in all spaces in our home space and our workspace, even in our outdoor space as AI goes global. All forms of this future of AI exist today. All—including you—are getting smarter and faster. Human adventure has never been more filled with hope and promise. Trust me on that possibility. Feast in the SUPER CHANGE. Bask in it. We created it all.

Some SUPER CHANGE challenges are more complex and require new learned behaviors to reach ideal solutions. In my book, *Redemption: The Cooperation Revolution*, I introduced the notion that competitive thought represents a droplet of pure concentrated evil and is not survivable as a thought form. Competition is the single-source virus of all human misery. It hides, as all viruses of the mind do, inside collective human consciousness. Competition is the First Insanity. Competition is the cause of misery in the home and workspaces of our lives. Cooperation is the cure. Competition is the source of workspace misery, parenting stress, and all relationships' lack of harmony. The reformed education on thinking is replacing insane, competitive thought expressions with integrity in self-dealing and self-talk, as well as integrity in all third-party undertakings. I will refuse to cooperate with you if you breach the integrity between us. The great work by Dr. David Gruder, *The New IQ: How Integrity Intelligence Serves You, Your Relationships, and Our World*, is the super glue that holds cooperation intact as your new whole-brain dominant thought. You alone control your own mind. *The New IQ* is a SUPER CHANGE tool kit for those wishing to live in communities without drama, inside integrity-based cooperation. Heaven is integrity and unconditional cooperation. Hell is no integrity and never-ending competition. Moving forward, you choose your own circle by making decisions. Heaven or hell. You get to choose. No one else can choose for you. Once you choose, you get what you chose.

Old Brains that embrace competitive insanity have no future in the age of SUPER CHANGE. No life of significance. No life of relevance. Cooperation and collaboration are the foundation of the happy, switched-on, turned-on home space, workspace and people space in the new age of SUPER CHANGE. This is the best brain "happy state" in both the present and the future. A better future for families, communities, institutions, ventures, states and nations is evolving from SUPER CHANGE, and soon AI will evolve into cooperative, rather than competitive, organization theory. Competitive thought is the source of all that holds human beings back. Cooperation is the one and only tool to remove the mental virus of competition at the core of our individual quantum computers. Only you have access to your *core* and can make the upgrade. You might ask yourself if you are willing to let competition go. When? How? *Will you?*

If you are Christian, embrace the reality that competition is Satan. Ancient texts do not contain the word "Satan." They call the evil "first competition with God." We lost its real name, for evil has a name, and it is "competitive thought impulse to elevate the ego"—that is, in fact, not even real. *That* is the true name of the insanity in free will first competition. Now that you know, move away from insanity. You alone control your mind.

Competition is neither good nor goodness, nor does it come from God. It comes from the first choice of free will—your first free will state— as you live and become alive. So you must choose to be insane or sane.

Your state of core being is your first choice.

Sanity is unconditional cooperation, collaboration and love. Being in that state is to exist in the pure holiness of all spirits in any faith or belief system. Competition is weakness and cooperation is strength. Competition is force, where cooperation is power. Power always removes force from the equation over time. Competition exists in judgment, blame and never-ending punishment of others. Cooperation exists in unconditional acceptance, love, tolerance, and cooperation without condition, or a state of heaven known as pure bliss. You alone choose the state within which you will keep your mind, noting the competition epidemic is viral within collective consciousness and re-infects wirelessly. Did you not know that? In the new age of SUPER CHANGE, your brain requires new firewalls to know that it has a competitive virus, and to block it from becoming active as you remove it from your system over time. Competition is insane in the home or workspace with all the predictable pain and suffering insanity always delivers as a consequence.

Insanity is where one infected mortal being competes with a divine immortal being at any level, which is itself first insanity for life. As a thought form, this is now self-evident. Insanity—competitive thought— is contagious, much like the flu. You can re-catch it. You can become re-infected. Your ego is always a magnet for insanity, especially in groups as they make you feel safe while judging and blaming other immortal spirits. Misery loves company.

It is true that insanity *is* misery. Misery in family. Misery in the workspace. Misery in community, nation, and even faith. Begin to see competitive thought impulses as a form of insanity. Catch this impulse and tell it to *go to its room*: it is like a 7-year-old that never grows into maturity.

However, you, the mature adult, can take charge of your future. Find a cooperative solution that is unconditionally collaborative. Leave all competitive distrust and win/lose negotiations out of your approach to future actions and decision-making. Before you lash out at anything—in your need to be *right* that is demonstrated by declaring any other divine immortal soul as being *wrong*—know that this virus "tendency" is the insanity of competition at work. So please, pause and just say to yourself, *how might I approach this cooperatively? What other course of action can I take to encourage the other party to join me in a desirable result? How can I talk without making them wrong in any way? What can I say that will make them feel safe?* If you are dealing with insane, unteachable brains, forgive them and remove yourself from their company. They are doing the best their spirit knows how to do. It is all ok. You may not be their teacher. They may be so infected they are not teachable. A good model for tools and tactics resides in my book *Perfection Can Be Had: My Father's Stories* within the story of the fairies and the boulder. Remember, this tool and tactic, if you acquire that work, was a modeling tool my famous father used on his children to firewall my nine siblings into heaven on Earth. And we did it.

SUPER CHANGE will then transmit even more software upgrades to your wetware. Either you will lead in SUPER CHANGE or you will bleed and be a victim of SUPER CHANGE. How you deal with SUPER CHANGE defines your success or failure in life—your forward adaptation is required to be successful. C-suite engagements are reviewing the criteria set forth here to engage long-term relationships with SUPER CHANGE brains at the top. Those who fail to adapt their thinking in communities facing SUPER CHANGE will be deleted. These deletions are occurring much more rapidly as weak brains who fail to upgrade their software are marginalized in career paths. They are less valuable.

How are you embracing or resisting SUPER CHANGE right now? Do you wish to upgrade your skills to embrace SUPER CHANGE? Is becoming current and relevant in a SUPER CHANGE age a priority for you right now? What is your misery index for failing to be current in the SUPER CHANGE age? What does your competitive misery index look like versus a cooperative joy index where your thinking is virus-free? Measure and assess yourself for a moment.

Come from the perspective of *I*, and never *you*. In a conversation, ask, "I loved what you just shared with me. I would have heard your mentorship even more powerfully if this were included. Does that resonate in any way?" Never say *you* as it feels like criticism and a threat to the emotional capital of humans. "Am I correct or off with what I heard?" You will be stunned by the person's reply as they reframe what you heard into what they actually meant. Always say, "Did you take my input as a plus and, if not, may I reframe, as I only meant it as a pure plus to our sharing together." This always makes input safe to the other party. We call this The Check. You can get to clarity collaboratively when you come from "what I heard" was x, y, and z, and "I ask" for clarification on a point or two. This is radically different from, "but you said this or that," and then having them snap back, "No I didn't," even while you are sure you heard them correctly. Alternatively, "I find what *you said* did not resonate with me or the group because *you* need to say this or that, this way or that way. Do you see what *you* have done here?" Any of that fails in transmission in SUPER CHANGE today.

A SUPER CHANGE technique we use at CEO Space is we ask CEOs to Check. The Check asks the party to restate what the desired outcomes are. The Check uncovers where there is a lack of agreement or correct understanding. The host then asks, "May I reframe those deliverables a bit? I have us almost united but needing a bit more." With permission, reframe the deliverables, and the understanding desired tends to flow where both parties feel safe in the exchange— no competition, no threat.

When the other party has outcomes precisely matching your own, reward them with a high five or more and suggest, "Now we are completely together in absolute clarity on that topic. Thank you so much."

This is a superior cooperative outcome to institutionalizing misunderstandings. Anyone receiving input in SUPER CHANGE cultures may state, without ramifications of any kind, "I did *not* take that as a plus." The party interpreted the input as competitive and negative to outcomes desired. The CEO or leaders then state, "May I reframe?" After which they inquire, "Did you take that as a *plus* rather than a criticism, as I meant it?" Now? The Check and monitoring of all requests for future outcomes is delivered, ensuring that the input was a *plus*. Again, the intuition, expectation, and the anticipatory set of competition is not present, and cooperation defines the superior experience between parties. Correction should always be a *plus*, and always in person.

Another tool and tactic:

Digital communication is for praise, and correction involves emotional context that requires positive leadership emotions to elevate mentors and improve outcomes without threat.

By asking for clarification, you see their mind did not mean what their words stated. When someone lashes out at you or escalates a situation, say to them, "Can you please restate what you just heard me say to you? I want to be clear on what you heard me say." Here is another way of coming from *I*: "I may have miscommunicated without any intention of doing so. Can you please tell me what I said to you to help me better understand any trigger or resistance I created, as it was fully not intended? Tell me." Again, you will be stunned at their reply. The escalation can then be reset when you say: "Gosh I had no idea you heard *that* from me—I made a huge communication error.

May I reframe what I was trying to say? Let's check what you heard before we start taking future action. I want to make sure you hear what I meant to communicate. Let me go long-form versus short-form, as that is my bad. You and I are bigger than any miscommunication."

SUPER CHANGE corrections praise all the contributions. SUPER CHANGE corrections never judge or blame when attempting to reframe outcomes to higher quality result. Outcomes are not personal. Fail to use the word "you" when creating interactions in SUPER CHANGE. Use "I," e.g., "I want to reward the outcomes you gave to us. I wish to strive to some outcome improvements with zero critique to your great, even outstanding, work. I want you to join me in seeing how outcomes can rise with your teamwork beside my own, if that works for us, and I want your full input on these suggestions." It works for *me* as a leader in my 150-nation CEO Space institution. These resets of cue language create improved workspace performance cultures—cultures that keep improving inside SUPER CHANGE.

This form of what I call "cue language" is a revolution in human relationships in our new digital age. Cue language applies to home, work, civic communities, and faith realms. Use "The Check"—a check-in to ask "What did you hear me say?"—as a powerful cooperative tool. Do not assume you are as clear as you think you are when seeking agreement from any other multi-tasking human being. This approach will do more to provide heaven on Earth than almost any other relationship tool you can engage. Monitor and measure your results.

Keep in your mind that brain synapse structures of those raised in, or adapting to, digital interactions, measured on MRIs (and we have them, believe me), are new and different from prior generations (your iPhone will report on the thousands of times, not hundreds, you pick up your smart phone a day). Psychologists will report that your brain chemistry response is similar to a sexual gratification response to digital stimulations. This reinforces entirely new synapse pathways. This now means that humans can pay attention, but they no longer can *continue* to pay attention without new cue language. Why? Because brains are click-and-scan conditions. We click and scan conversations and hear only fragments due to our digitally fragmented attention. We now multi-task inside our brains even when present with other human beings. We are slowly placing more value on superficial digital conversation over real human relationships. This is making us *over-stressed* and starving for real relationships. Listening is now a cue language itself, as we are all starving to be truly "well heard" with one another. In this rapidly changing brain chemistry, with newly designed brain chemistry drugs coming to manipulate every mood and focus soon, new humans are cheating nature and tens of millions of years of evolution. AI and technology are allowing us to evolve at speeds never known before. We are evolving ourselves with digital, artificial, and addicting stimulations. Steve Jobs rationed his children's iPhone time, telling them, hey, we designed it to be fully addicting.

Where this is all going, no one knows. Digitally conditioned brains—the majority of humans today—require a new cue language at work and in the home to elevate human-to-human relationships that are non-digital. You cannot scan and delete your wife, children or co-workers, so do not try. Super Focus is the new human essential IQ into the future. Click the link below for a digital super focus tool we define as a new SUPER CHANGE asset to restore brain super focus with new digitally effected synapse brain patterns unfolding www.eyeq. com. I suggest you buy this product for your entire employee teams worldwide for instant performance gains in the cue language that all digital brains require. CEO Space offers the only keynotes and trainings of which we know related to new cue language in the workspace.

Now that you can discern who is who (sane or insane), your life will never be the same. However, keep in mind that the sane can also never teach the insane, for they are not teachable. Besides, you were never their teacher anyway. As you share SUPER CHANGE, you ensure that those you love and for whom you care will have the tools to know and understand the age in which we reside—the SUPER CHANGE age. Embrace it.

Insane brains or brains infected with competitive software discuss never-ending blame games for people, places and things in which they are the true heroes in judgment of others. Insane brains are *past dwellers* looped in discussions that are focused on the past three months of memory.

Sane brains super focus on creating forward solutions, and they dwell on future talk, focusing on the hope and promise they are creating in the future. Sane brains reframe from blame, judgment and past-dwelling mind focus. Sane brains listen but never buy in. They listen in silence to competitive marked circles they cannot influence, teach, or elevate. Sane brains experience insanity as pain. Sane brains remove over-stress and insanity pain by residing in circles with other sane brains. Using SUPER CHANGE processes to remain with self-correcting, virus-free brains, they circle with sane brain communities. They guard these community associations, which self-correct one another, as *plussing* always with a Check—"Did you take that as a *plus*?" They guard the guards.

Where are you living life? Insane brains reside in, "There must be more to life than this."

Sane brains reside in gratitude, acknowledgement and appreciation in lives that absolutely *thrill* them, without exception.

Guess what? You were born to choose your own circle. Your own life. So, choose, but with caution. Once you know you are sane, you can still be re-infected. So, guard your circle and guard your guards like Napoleon Hill. In Napoleon Hill's last and most important work, *Outwitting the Devil*, he predicts living in cooperation in 1937, and instructs us to guard our circle and guard the guards. Thank *you*, Uncle Nappy, for mentoring a young boy who had no clue about the magic software you upgraded into his brain over those many years.

CHAPTER 2

LEADERS ON THE WATCH

I'VE HAD THE PLEASURE OF being the chairman of the world's highest press-ranked entrepreneurial global conference, CEO Space International. We serve 150 nations and are now starting our fourth decade of public service to leaders. Before then, my twenty-two years as chairman of a public, global investment banking institution with a reach from Wall Street to Paris, created a dark hole in my economist soul. I was in pain over the broken, competitive, capitalist financial system. In all context assessments, this corrupt, competitive capitalism (a system of *the few against the many*) requires reform to contribute to our better welfare. The same held true for the even greater failure of socialist and communist competitive systems, even worse than the failures of competitive capitalism and its failed rule sets. AI is already changing everything in our new decades. We now reside in a new economic system of AI capitalism that the world has yet to understand.

Prosperity, in SUPER CHANGE, harbors the most important economic revolution of all time: the transformation of failed *competitive* capitalism, socialism, and communism, into a global *cooperative* capitalism that self-corrects and precludes integrity breakdown. My book, *Redemption: The Cooperation Revolution*, was designed to be a GPS for national leaders, corporate leadership in venture space, as well as Fortune 500 C-suite planners seeking to reform their economic systemic models into cooperative capitalism.

SUPER CHANGE is a shift I observed up-close-and-personal from Wall Street. It is a long road from the days of David Rockefeller or Bill Witter, where a handshake created contracts that never wavered, to today's signed contracts whose dried ink still often only means, "We are just starting to negotiate." I saw between the 1960s and the 1980s a global market space where ninety percent of all global investment was stakeholder trading (owning a stock or bond). Compare this to 2020, where ninety-nine percent of current stakeholder trading is manipulated and market price "fixed" through side bets on which way an asset might go in the future. This is the same casino capitalism subscribed to in the 1929 Great Depression. Speculation and wealth consolidations became an upside-down pyramid to global liquidity flows and it is worse today as it is all digital and AI. This new form of unregulated AI casino economics is new to humanity and includes second-by-second volume trades on future prices of coffee, livestock, steel, copper, oil, wheat and even national currencies.

Side bets today have totally rigged and destroyed the world capital market space. They are criminal-like levels of unregulated capital flows controlled now by AI, not humans, as money is leveraged and borrowed in ratios the world has never before experienced. This mayhem is made possible by competitive, central banking-based, free money policy that will, if left unchecked, open the door for the greatest depression and world war of human history. This criminal, global greed machine should have been regulated out of existence.

On Wall Street, I saw regulations that stayed in place for more than 100 years—regulations designed by very smart economic post-Depression brains set and designed to be our global safety net—get voted out by an unaware congress and rendered meaningless. As the old regulations of seventy years evaporated in 2000, no new regulatory framework envisioning, say, a rapidly unfolding AI new world economy, was even on the drawing board of nations. I saw regulations, at the local level, lose all relevance because the early days of the digital SUPER CHANGE market moved all the trades into the cloud where there was no nation or law or AI to manage AI in new models of global cloud-based financial regulation. Shadow banking and unregulated dark pools now dominate the rigged global market space. Now is the time to initiate a global digital-age regulatory "re-think." AI is now controlling 440 trillion trading capital flows worldwide without human oversight or any nation's regulations. We are in a new casino capitalism where all bets are managed by AI rather than humans for the first time in history. The shift occurred too rapidly for human systems, law making or regulatory agencies to adapt—2015 to 2018. In three years, AI bypassed five thousand years of human economic history. A new global AI, an unregulated AI economy, is now in control of capital flows to all nations and markets. The danger of casino capitalism has yet to come to the light of lawmakers and regulators. Today, upgraded regulations must be G100 Global and engage AI to moderate greed and system abuse. The roaring abuse today is unwanted wealth consolidation where one percent own more wealth (fewer than ten thousand super money pools) than the remaining ninety-nine combined. This is not sustainable economics. SUPER CHANGE has struck economics globally. Catching up will be difficult because the pace of change is accelerating too fast for human systems to upgrade into SUPER CHANGE AI economics.

Until a global G100 re-regulation occurs, the foundation of free capital markets is now entrenched in casino capitalism, with no regulatory controls to serve as a safety net against an utter collapse of the core system. The "too big to jail" era has arrived—with its multi-million dollar fines that are considered a cost of doing business in this new era of economic casino capitalism. As there is no global consequence for stealing tens of billions, this criminal casino is rapidly evolving, resulting in criminal titans ripping off everyone else—the system of *the few against the many*, which is always corrupt, insane, and competitive. It is a world of AI software evolving, quarter to quarter, within trillions of investment dollars, against AI software that is part of a brand-new economic history for national planners.

The IMF, the World Bank, and economists like me in my blog www.bernydohrmann.com, have warned for decades against this unregulated new economy. We accurately predicted the 1973 oil embargo; the Reagan Recession; the 9/11 recession; the 2008 Big Short and recession; and now the *super crash* about to thunder down upon the out-of-control deflationary markets caused by Super Debt Bubbles in the EU and Asia, if we are not very careful. SUPER CHANGE is unforgiving to those behind the acceleration and change. We believe SUPER CHANGE economics, with AI economies now in control, is the first priority of global lawmakers to re-engineer the safety net for the world.

We have seen communism lose all control of its markets when the digital speculators' market space unleashed itself outside of any regulatory box. We have seen the Gulf lose control over OPEC, oil, and other commodities. We have seen capitalist markets and regulators lose control as economics moved to the cloud as regulations became increasingly isolated and localized. Today, the market trades without any form of national or global supervision. All such super leverage would be considered illegal in almost any nation, but there is no social basis for casino capitalism's AI speculations that robs nations of their ability to plan and prosper. The current global world order is failing to adapt in a new syndrome we label SUPER CHANGE disorder.

We have seen legal *and* illegal theft from *nations* go beyond anything known in any prior age. One hundred million dollars, for example, was stolen from *one* Asian bank in a single hack. It was blocked on its way to being ten *billion* dollars due to only a single typing error by the crooks. We have seen sixteen million dollars in oil payments evaporate from Nigeria—Price Waterhouse says that may represent only the tip of Nigeria's lack of integrity and morality. We have seen one hundred *trillion* dollars in bad debts through failed national policies from China to the EU to the USA. Yet none of those one hundred trillion dollars has worked its way through the failed competitive, capitalist, socialist, or communist models. In 2019, two top-100 China public firms lost six billion dollars of cold hard cash on their books, and auditors have no clue where the *six billion dollars* evaporated to, so complete was the digital evaporation of record history by the criminal public leadership. China regulatory agencies had no clue, as their oversight in new AI economics is decades behind the SUPER CHANGE.

Most of the non-performing loans (bad debt) are still carried as good assets on institutional balance sheets worldwide, but mostly in China; an historic super China debt bomb spiraling ever upward, where China spends three hundred percent more than it earns. That was a crime under old laws, but it is not a crime under new laws. Additional trillions are invested every month on ever-smarter AI than any other economic flow of capital upon the Earth today. All AI inventing takes place inside a mindless race, where the winner will control the entire world. This AI arms race is the defining evolution of humanity, all taking place without a G100 game plan, regulatory framework, or sense of controlled outcome. Humans took some time to discover if you play with fire long enough you will get burned. SUPER CHANGE is the sun versus a welding torch.

Guess what? My readers, at one level or another, know this risk and understand the implications. In fact, my readers know more than lawmakers who wish to keep the mantra, "No change on my watch," or worse, "That's the way we have always done it." That is the fatal mental software loop. Lawmakers need a *process* to become and remain current in SUPER CHANGE. Each two-year election, I have thought a four-day SUPER CHANGE experience from CEO Space, the accredited faculty of which law firms lawmakers respect, would do the trick for incoming lawmakers and their staff. Wealth consolidation—AI economics and fantastic debt margin and leverage in the system—is creating inflated artificial values in everything. SUPER CHANGE has left nations and regulatory agencies behind. The rising danger is if we fail to *re*-regulate the AI landscape of SUPER CHANGE. I vote for humanity. We can catch up quickly.

Activities at these levels were impossible before SUPER CHANGE. Schoolchildren in Chicago have been beaten to death because they refused to share their chewing gum while walking to school in the morning. A woman and man—each only seventeen years old—were stoned to death for daring to love each other outside their families' arranged marriage under culture and faith. Individual freedom, choice and love were punished by buggy, awful, "culture competitive" brain software instead of celebrated. Those doing the stoning cannot recall who loaded that godawful software into their young brains that permitted stoning their own children to death. Is a G100 Earth Federation "common" law to better navigate SUPER CHANGE not a matter of some urgency when you think about it?

As all laws are local and AI is in the cloud, a G100 global regulatory outcome is desired with a cooperative basis so that no nation will be left behind when implemented. SUPER CHANGE calls for lawmakers to read up on the options. Read *Redemption: The Cooperation Revolution*. Institutional leaders, before you pack up your flavor of 2020, send these books to your lawmakers, staff and your candidates. Work toward upgrading software for us all.

An underdeveloped city in a fractured region has gone from three million inhabitants to ten million in only four years due to mass migrations. This city needs assistance in supplying adequate food, healthcare, shelter, education, rule of law, childcare, schools, transportation, water, and electricity. Not even in World War II—not *ever*—has regional war contributed to such mass migrations still going on in the EU and Gulf. When zero resources exist, how does a nation, already hampered by recession and buried in obligations to pay off all of the EU's debt by itself, all while holding another hundred trillion dollars in bad EU non-paying debts, provide for a new city that large with language and culture issues that impact the effort in the first place? Economically speaking, it is impossible.

We have seen unfunded pension obligations for USA civic institutions pass one hundred billion dollars in shortfall in a single year, with no equitable way to close this "entitlement" funding gap. This funding gap globally exceeds another one hundred trillion dollars in shortfall. In what economic system is this deficit in funding made whole? We know of none. We have seen more and more institutions, cities, states and nations go entirely bankrupt worldwide. This first in history is now occuring across the world. Did you see that as a SUPER CHANGE problem? If we lie to our nations, we imprisoned as felons. If the nations lie to us, however, it is called "politics." It seems that people in power lie and tell us everything is OK—not to worry—because, in competitive systems, no one is held accountable for breaches in core integrity. In cooperative systems, where integrity is the binding agency, crimes are crimes and there is no "get out of jail free" card.

The media is owned by less than fifty super wealthy individuals. AI now data points audience demographics. News is now tailored for a specific audience. Filtered. The safeguard for informed voters has moved from news to fake news. Stormy Daniels did "x" with President Trump—Stormy, after making big bucks, states, "No, that was all wrong—never happened." Take it from that level into everything else. We are becoming distrustful of all media today and consider it biased. Media is manipulating voters and the public. AI now is brainwashing *us* with information for profit. That is new. We can roll back the tide but we must rise over the top of competitive spirals of greed and the crisis created by brains infected with competition. This is the crisis of integrity we are witnessing.

SUPER CHANGE and new AI is creating the end of the old "competitive" system world order, but speculation is creating the rise of a new AI—insane, economic, competitive modeling which is not yet sustainable. It is ushering in insane economics where the super wealthy get fantastically richer by manipulating the price of everything via hidden taxes on all nations and peoples using AI they paid for and control to enrich their already wealthy coffers. In the new AI digital age, nations have lost the regulatory control and integrity of their market places unregulated AI economic markets of the new age of SUPER CHANGE.

The only way for today's unregulated super AI speculation in economics to be regulated again would be with reforms designed at a G100 economic constitutional convention hosted over three years to retool global, legal, and regulatory AI frameworks. The trades are global and cloud-based, so laws must be global and G100 inclusive by treaty to re-regulate in SUPER CHANGE. It is there that we could forge a new, global, regulatory trade scheme as well as a universal set of regulatory laws in which no nation is left behind. Can we do better? You bet we can, we should, and we must, as yesterday *is* already too late for eight billion of us on system core stability facing SUPER CHANGE in economics. The risk is a system crash in which leaders bemoan, "Oh, how did this take place?" when it took place due to failure to take appropriate remedial action. Cooperative capitalism reforms would ensure that system corruption would be shut down. System survival can be salvaged, but time in AI time frames is drawing to a close... for humanity to act.

However, an inclination to cooperate, to solve the problem, is derailed by the fear and distrust inherent in the current competitive, integrity-free, leader mindset model. The minds of leadership, as you see, are infected with the competitive virus. In the entrenched super-competitive political models, everyone is looking out for their own interests, even when those interests are against the common collective good. A system where one percent own more wealth than ninety-nine percent is not sustainable. A system of *the few against the many* is never sustainable. Together, we all win, or, by moving apart, we lose together. SUPER CHANGE leaders might look at source cause versus symptoms, as inspired leadership in the SUPER CHANGE option you now understand more clearly to choose sanity. The others (insane competitive brains) will die off. As more global voters read and share SUPER CHANGE, the voters will reveal the Old Brains that are unteachable.

Cooperation is a permanent solution, but competition is temporary.

I see genocide and weapons of mass destruction—coupled to war crimes not seen since World War II—on evening, dinnertime news, as our collective world splits into mindsets of competition or cooperation. Meanwhile, real criminals behead their own mothers and call it the master faith in crazy brain competition, as usual. If I had told families in 1965 what SUPER CHANGE in 2030 would look like, they would have locked me up as insane. Yet, everyone who is looking toward 2030 today can see the pure insanity of it. When all eight billion of us, with few exceptions, just trust, love, and cannot wait to learn from each other in natural cooperation, respect and integrity, the great majority of us will not be insane.

You either choose leadership that will lead, or bleed, in SUPER CHANGE. What is your capacity to adapt? Some of the template rules that will keep you current—meaning you manage your brain software to become and remain SUPER CHANGE current—include the following:

CURRENCY TOOLS AND TACTICS TO UPGRADE YOUR MIND:

Schedule time to do online research of worldwide SUPER CHANGE. Locate various global news sources and scan them many times a week. And, as always, follow the money. Guard the seeds you put in your mind. Read more. Turn off the television. Subscribe to the SUPER CHANGE leaders site www.bernydohrmann.com as a leading source that is always free.

Choose your mentors more carefully. Circle with those ahead in SUPER CHANGE such as innovators, creators, and leaders focused on cooperation. Avoid competitive followers and communities, and remain free of slow adapters to SUPER CHANGE. Changing your circle can improve your ability to adapt to SUPER CHANGE. Protect your circle as SUPER CHANGE thinkers, and then *guard your guards*. Competitive infected virus brains will try to get into protected cooperative leadership circles, just as the moth in the woods is attracted to the light in the meadow. *Your life transforms as you transform your circle. Choose mentors who are SUPER CHANGE all-stars. Change two mentors, triple your income, and double your time off.*

Research and invest in the best-of-the-best live trainings that can keep you current in SUPER CHANGE. We recommend George Frasier's *Power Networking* event, as well as events by Tony Robbins, Greg Reid, Sharon Lechter, and our own CEO Space, to name a few. Check out some of our CEO Space Faculty, all vetted online (www.ceospaceinterntional.com) from Adam Markel to Daniel Ruke at Blink as SUPER CHANGE mentors, like Harry Lay. Check that out at CEO Space as a resource in SUPER CHANGE that leads to other resources, all vetted by third parties so that you can trust our alliance endorsements. From Jack Canfield of the *Chicken Soup for the Soul* series, to Bob Proctor of *Paradigm Shift* (which was birthed at CEO SPACE), pick your ribbons on the SUPER CHANGE Maypole and dance for success in upgraded leadership outcomes. Pick one new SUPER CHANGE mentor, including me (256-850-4715 to explore my mentorship offers), and dive into currency in SUPER CHANGE. Every brain needs upgraded software, given the pace of change. What is your process?

For business owners, know that your customers are mind-shifting. Are they more or less confident today than ten years ago? Are they more or less afraid? Are you tracking your own patterns and trends daily? Are you slow to keep pace with your customers, or teammates, or family partners' ever-shifting mindsets?

As markets shift, how does your value proposition match with your customers' actual mindsets, or does it simply match with your own obsolete SUPER CHANGE thinking and thought patterns? Why they buy is far more important than how you sell to them. Cheri Tre is a CEO Space faculty leader and full-blast SUPER CHANGE leader. Read her book, *Why They Buy.* I recommend Cheri's program as yet another SUPER CHANGE process for my readers seeking a process to bring them current and keep them current. For our process, Google "CEO Space Bob Proctor on change," and "CEO Space Les Brown on SUPER CHANGE." There, you will find short, powerful, information for leader upgrading.

When your stakeholders are afraid, you need to be dollar and price-point conscious to inspire and to gain trust for repeat buying and loyalty in fast-changing SUPER CHANGE markets. Never in history have market mindsets shifted so rapidly, all connected to mind-manipulating news controlled by the fewer than ten thousand super money pool CEOs we call "The Owners." The Owners of what? The owners of everything. When your customer mindsets are more confident, you need to inspire value-based features to drive new cycle changes toward your desired outcomes. Security in any cycle is brief—what once lasted three years now lasts three *months,* if you are lucky.

Today, we know that accelerated SUPER CHANGE *is* the new normal.

Product cycles, once sixty months, are now sixty weeks.

We all need to calm down to catch up. We need to think differently. We need to calm down and become far more objective about what we are seeing, hearing, reading, and using to make decisions. We need to re-train ourselves because the leadership skill of the century has become your process to adapt to SUPER CHANGE. Leaders who demonstrate flexible thinking, the ability to learn-unlearn-relearn, and welcome diverse mindsets will thrive in the new SUPER CHANGE market space. Futurist Alvin Toffler first released the mind software master skill for SUPER CHANGE when he stated that education in the future is brains that learn faster, unlearn even faster, and relearn fastest. Those are the leaders who are priceless decision-makers moving forward.

So, whom are you hiring? Which leader are YOU? Do you even know?

CHAPTER 3

HOW YOU FIND OUT

BEFORE SUPER CHANGE, YOU MAY HAVE had the notion that you would be equal in brand weight if you created a web presence like that of Fortune brands. However, technology is changing at a pace beyond any human experience. Not too long ago, we were born into an "age." The earlier ages defined your social position for generations, and everyone knew his or her station. You saw hundreds upon hundreds of years in the Iron Age, the Bronze Age, and the Stone Age. Generations were clear about the social strata within which they resided. You were a mason or a silversmith by guild and family and heritage. This defined your life and station in society. No SUPER CHANGE at all. *Game of Thrones* reminded us of one era of slower-paced change.

There was a calm, collective, peaceful, *knowing,* related to your social position—from owner to slave, for example—across all the ages. In fact, the idea that slavery was wrong—and violated a basic human right—is *new* in human experience. All our prior generations were either masters or slaves, depending which side won the war. Slavery included all races and cultures—to the victor went the spoils. Then SUPER CHANGE came along, revolutionized old human thinking, and all that positioning shifted. Slavery was seen as insane, a criminal violation of human rights. SUPER CHANGE is the agency of transformation and it is all taking place in the "mind field."

Suddenly, in a single generation's time, we've moved from the Industrial Age; through the automobile age; the age of flight; the atomic age; the jet age; the space age; the moon landing age; the information age; the computer and internet age; the communication age; the entrepreneur age; the age of AI economics unfolding today, to now the first stable age in one hundred years: the age of SUPER CHANGE.

The velocity of change—the acceleration of change—is so dramatic that the future may belong to AIs and genetically improved trans-humans. They will be a new, super, "class set" of life and likely foster capabilities, unknown to the intelligence we possess today, that will thrive and propel SUPER CHANGE even further. The pace of our adaptation is challenging for us, but we still need to prosper and thrive inside the age of unfolding SUPER CHANGE. We were born into this age and we cannot get out of SUPER CHANGE now. The pace of SUPER CHANGE is moving in only one direction.

AI fuels an explosive pace of acceleration to SUPER CHANGE, which has already reached the human capacity for adaption. Are we reaching a red line as humans which we simply cannot cross?

In this book, the tools and tactics to prosper in SUPER CHANGE are presented for the first time with cooperation and love for each of you. Know that you are the hope and promise for all of our tomorrows, one mind at a time. You are indeed the hope and the promise of the entire world as you move to embrace and master SUPER CHANGE because... you can do it.

For larger institutions seeking a process for SUPER CHANGE in team performance elevations, allow me to recommend Les Purdew. Purdew's website www.purdewprinciple.com is filled with proofs of his game theory for teams in larger workspaces. As a CEO Space faculty leader, Les executes The Escape Room using game theory to reform brain software in teams. Because the only way out of the escape room is to cooperate, and no amount of competition can get team members out, the effects are lasting. The brain new software of using cooperation to problem solve is immediate and long lasting. CEO Space and The Escape Room are two institutional processes that work quickly. CEO Space requires a week off-site at our hosting locations every sixty days, or five times a year, for teams and leadership upgrading. Les Purdew's Escape Room comes to your divisions across the world and works in a short time to upgrade performance outcomes, thereby fostering massive new creative problem solving abilities. Nothing else comes close as a SUPER CHANGE agency for Fortune institutions and their peers.

The future of education will be defined by New Brains that foster cultures of SUPER CHANGE leadership inside education. Education will advance core skills of thinking processes that accommodate and embrace our era of SUPER CHANGE. It will foster facilities that accelerate innovation and change that we cannot yet imagine. The new math is 1+1 = 11, not 2. Synergistic, cooperative, organizational theory engages us all *and* is presently a desert inside conventional global education. As escape rooms come to Harvard and Stanford, faculty will upgrade to embrace, rather than resist, SUPER CHANGE and lead educational reform, or others (like Keiser University, who already are) will take over at the helm. Art Keiser and Belinda are examples of an institutional embrace of SUPER CHANGE, as well as their President in 2020, Gary Volk, a CEO Space member.

Systemic organization reforms inside education define the institution's prospects to thrive or die in the future of the SUPER CHANGE market space. Reform your workspace and home space game until 1 + 1 SUPER CHANGE brains equal 11 as a result of our upgraded brains working together. Working with AI and AI working with *us*. If only laws and policies would foster this union to embrace SUPER CHANGE, we would have more certainty moving forward.

New laws must foster acceleration into SUPER CHANGE, and never work to slow or resist SUPER CHANGE. Such efforts would be like trying to stop a glacier moving to the sea using a screwdriver.

Wrong tool. You cannot stop a hurricane with a ceiling fan. Wrong tool. Embrace SUPER CHANGE—you cannot stop it and you cannot slow it down. Join SUPER CHANGE and become fully engaged as a competent human leader and adapter.

Mastermind thinking will rule the education in the C-suites of tomorrow. Cooperative versus competitive teams and mastermind circles will creatively solve future challenges. SUPER CHANGE principles and tools will rule the C-suite leadership teams that advance acceleration of prosperity in institutional management. *Change will only accelerate.* The pace of change will advance levels of thought heretofore unavailable to humanity over hundreds of thousands of years.

Transformation of pyramid competitive management theory into "hub wagon wheel" cooperative management theory will advance at levels which will revise corporate cultures worldwide in a single generation. The old competitive models of industry and nations will be seen as inefficient, toxic, and wasteful. Competitive organizational theory will fall into the trash bin of failed human rulesets that resulted in *Westworld* and *The Game of Thrones* or *Terminator* as the outcome of the competitive insanity virus on brains.

Virus-free cooperative brains will flourish in the new integrity and cooperation-based new models defined by publications like *People Over Profit* by Dale Partridge. Read *Busting Loose from the Money Gang* by Robert Scheinfeld to work on your brain software upgrade to become a master SUPER CHANGE adapter. *Busting Loose* presents mind-blowing strategies to bust free of the old top-down failed management rules of the money game that you can never win, from billionaire to millionaire. The SUPER CHANGE new box top rules that assure you win every single minute of your game board, in both money and success in life, is one book away. SUPER CHANGE adapters will all read *Busting Loose*. Trust me. Leaders are readers.

In a single generation, SUPER CHANGE has become the defining age by which your future performance will be measured. Your capacity to thrive in SUPER CHANGE is your defining thought form, a metric for measuring your value and worth in both the present and the future marketplace. If you resist SUPER CHANGE, your market value is less. If you embrace SUPER CHANGE, you demonstrate your ability to learn faster, unlearn even faster, and relearn faster than ever. The marketplace elevates your value based on that new *flexible brain*.

It has become that simple, as boards, owners, and heads of practices increasingly hire those who have read SUPER CHANGE and aspire to *flexibrain* skills—to learn–unlearn–relearn faster than any prior generation of super computer: your brain. A growing number of influencers have attended CEO Space, from Accenture; Booz Allen and McKinsey; leading corporate trainers, like the best-of-the-best Tony Robbins; Cheri Hill; Sharon Lechter; Steve Farber; Robert Johnson of Duke affiliation; Retired Dean of UAH Dr. Wilson; Greg Reid of *Secret Knock*; Jack Canfield; Les Brown; Lisa Nichols; Mark Victor Hansen; Bill Walsh; James Dentley; and new leaders in corporate training attending to upgrade their own products into SUPER CHANGE. The trend is unstoppable. Tomorrow's leaders require a process that is ongoing to remain relevant to their stakeholders in ever-accelerating SUPER CHANGE.

You may become slightly annoyed with public education that still rewards the competitive model of mediocrity and the status quo, which, without weight, disregards ethics and integrity. This has become our current global social crisis of human excellence in accelerated terms. New institutions that understand and teach SUPER CHANGE are commanding billions in tuitions, while Ivy League schools are fighting for relevance in performance-based SUPER CHANGE markets. Adapt, and you will remain current and fully relevant. Fail to lead in SUPER CHANGE mental skill, and you are obsolete and no longer relevant to lead at all.

Higher income for life occurs from owning ventures or practices in the age of the entrepreneur, or being entrepreneurial with a SUPER

CHANGE brain in any career path. Tip: Increasingly avoid the misery of agreeing with or remaining in competitive obsolete career path systems. You are not a tree. You can move. You *are* the referee of your own life. Position your wealth—your life "time"—as an investment you pay to switched-on, turned-on SUPER CHANGE institutions. If you lead one, or wish to transform into one, take the following steps. First, ensure that all employees and suppliers read SUPER CHANGE. The difference will be electric. Second, ensure all silo leaders and managers read *Redemption: The Cooperation Revolution*. Third, outline from *Redemption* the system-wide leadership reform steps in the work, removing waste and low performance swamps as you explode performance and generate outcomes impossible without the culture reform.

Leaders are readers. You do not need to pay fortunes for management upgrading from outside firms that, frankly, apply obsolete tools that worked once upon a time. In my last conversations with Dr. Edward Demining and my famous father, from their hospital beds, they harped upon the conclusion, from data, that there *is* and *remains* in a magic hourglass an absolute ceiling for performance gains in competitive system engineering for an entity of any size. These two inventors and lifetime collaborators—cooperating in post-World War II eras when the world was compressing into competition—invented TQM, TVQM, Six Sigma and the IP that changed the corporate world into the world we all know today.

Their final work was to uncork unlimited human potential. This great "top of the hourglass" of human performance explosions took form in transforming cultures from *competitive* modeling into *cooperative* modeling. Today, their work, which inspired CEO Space corporate training, is revolutionizing the world all over again. Jeff Bezos, who created Amazon with the cooperative principles of SUPER CHANGE, the first trillion dollar institution before 2020, drives *Redemption* principles that include:

All our employees think like owners... We have no competition... All of us at Amazon are fully obsessed with how we can, in Super Focus, improve the experience of the customer we serve within the highest social good while making a profit... All our employees with an improvement idea may go over and around any supervisor, manager, vice president and myself as controlling shareholder, founder and CEO... In fact, I reward maximally any employee who will not give up on an idea that they just know will improve our results for our clients and customers...

Such principles of cooperative theory in management replace faulty, lower-performance, lower-integrity, lower-contributing social models. They are all failed system models of competitive pyramid organization theory still taught at virtually every MBA program in the world. One Fortune 100 Executive VP stated the hundreds of millions they invest in higher education are squandered, wasted dollars. It now takes more hundreds of millions and five years to hire university-damaged brains, to help those brains to learn the Fortune 100 culture model, to unlearn the bad university software, and to relearn what is truly required and desired in their workspaces. Flying across the USA recently, he stated, "The risk to our future in America is the risk we will fail to fully, from scratch, retool education to accommodate super change." There is much more to that story, but it confirms that you are ahead already by reading SUPER CHANGE today. Your social capital account is rising fast.

Let's go back to being online before SUPER CHANGE, in a time when you created a web page and did business. Today, you need to create a *supersite* that accommodates SUPER CHANGE. There are more than eight billion websites online at this instant. There are upwards of 150 million new websites coming online each month, and that number is soaring quarterly. Four billion humans are yet to be online at all worldwide. The existing sites are increasingly complex and interactive in virtual space. There are more sites on the internet than humans online. The largest income from online activity is pornography, sex and violent streaming games—which is also the largest US export. Shame on us all.

Having multiple websites means little in the SUPER CHANGE market space. There are more websites than there are humans online at any hour.

To win in online space, you must adjust the design of your supersite to incorporate ever-changing, advancing options of SUPER CHANGE, including:

- iWatch, and any equivalent wearable compatibility
- VR compatibility with each SUPER CHANGE advance in VR
- Plugin inclusions for user currency experiences
- Super Changing, lower cost, faster to you, pay inventions; Apple Pay was not here a short time back nor was blockchain.
- Currency itself—Blockchain and bio-ledger capabilities— the world is moving to lower cost in SUPER CHANGE, always
- Linked site communities and cross-shared affiliated sites
- Feeder strategies to feed warmed-up buyers to your web worlds
- Hurricane sites that pull in your ideal buyers by design
- Conversion sites (ninety percent are not) that, in fewer clicks, convert the ever-shorter *click attention* span to sales completions
- Three R sites that R-tain your client, R-peat buy your client, R-ferral reward your client
- Site wow factors by design, pre-sale reward (free?), at-sale reward and acknowledgement, and repeat buyer rewards built into SUPER CHANGE future sites.

- Gamification—fewer clicks and more fun, to keep your client happy and engaged, enjoying their experience compared to other placeholder sites
- Always improving, always upgrading, fresh and SUPER CHANGING by strategy
- New products featured and new services featured
- Endless sale and value featured
- 5G to 100G
- Animated 3D product
- Virtual shopping with a cart that fills as you go down virtual aisles instead of lines of type. You can't tell you're not in the store—items go in and out of the cart and the supplier delivers to you in an hour
- Interactive customer service—they see you, you see them—the customer service waits for the customer, your client never waits for the customer service. AI makes it all possible in SUPER CHANGE
- Using AI or not

What is your checklist for upgrading your website into SUPER CHANGE? The process to upgrade your brain software must be ongoing, regular, and consistent.

In 1988, CEO Space, stepping into the void of SUPER CHANGE for Fortune institutional management, started with institutions from 3M with Joan Gustafson, head of 3M training, which led to AT&T and to Zellerbach. Over time, in the entrepreneur age, CEO Space advanced access to small businesses and professionals who were missing Fortune-grade SUPER CHANGE tools and tactics. The concept then and the concept in 2050 is that we cannot anchor core skills by webinar or seminar. Thunderstorms of data raining into our awareness do not create new hard skills to act on in ever-higher performance outcomes. Humans must work where entire communities practice the new skills evolving in SUPER CHANGE under mentorship experts and skill transfer authorities, to elevate collective skills in industrial, national, and professional spaces. Humans require customization—your customized need in SUPER CHANGE is not the same as another industry silo. What is your customized process to continually advance SUPER CHANGE adaptation as the new need for leadership? Four days, every sixty days, or every 180? What is *your process*? Ours is CEO Space and we recommend our graduate programs as your alternative choice, because they all address the issues presented here. CEO Space uniquely includes families and children in very advanced leadership training. Again, ranked for ten years the number one business conference for the desired process outcomes by third-party press, as seen on our websites for your own exploration when the time is right for you.

Web resources need to SUPER CHANGE all the time.

Supersites are modeled to upgrade quarterly as obsolescence is now measured in months instead of years. Are *you* fully current online? A hurricane site sucks in your demographic customer base by large numbers and works to maximally convert those clicks to real sales. Leakage or "click waste" is monitored and declining. Everything less is what we call a placeholder site waiting to upgrade into a supersite. Firms like Blink in Orlando or Solution Stream in Salt Lake City (CEO Space leaders) produce supersite upgrades as endorsed SUPER CHANGE-leading web providers. Tracy Pyke does lower-cost solutions for smaller firms out of Atlanta at a quality we also endorse to our members and their teams. When exploring upgrades to underperforming web investments, or over-performing profit-making supersites, explore with these resources provided at a click, and ask them for their best endorsements. Shop, compare, and upgrade. SUPER CHANGE leaves those who delay behind forever *today*.

In the new age of SUPER CHANGE, you either *cash your brand* or you *trash your brand*. Time is your one asset that *is* more precious than diamonds. In SUPER CHANGE, delay to higher pay is the one price far too costly to pay. Upgrade to a SUPER CHANGE currency site that is always presenting new and fresh outcomes, promotions, and deals to your growing client base. Choose your own "click factor" for your choice of resources, as those SUPER CHANGE sites are growing and serving all cultures and languages. Online SUPER CHANGE communities celebrate diversity, bring us together, and self-regulate competitive brain removals from the social capital of your target community without judgment or blame. SUPER CHANGE mindsets are new, and all SUPER CHANGE brains know one another instantly. Look for them and associate with future talkers versus past gossipers.

C-suite leaders transitioning from Old Brain software to New Brain software are stretched because they lack SUPER CHANGE models for their future coping strategy. The first mark of leadership in the SUPER CHANGE space is like a relay race, where leadership passes batons at every turn in their private track, issuing ever-more-current, inspired, and fresh management adjustments in their spaces. Reward and recognize SUPER CHANGE brains for using SUPER CHANGE as a cultural model for planning strategies and improved endgame decision-making. C-suite leaders must be vetted in order to remain progressive, to learn-unlearn-relearn (as new C-suite culture policy), and, in general, to lead in the future age of SUPER CHANGE. Cooperative cultures are required to lead in SUPER CHANGE. Unreformed Old Brain competitive cultures are either dying or engaging culture reform experts to retool their failing competitive culture—like Sears compared to a cooperative culture such as Amazon or Pinterest.

While competitive cultures revolve around the principles of fear, punishment, and exploitation within an antique, pyramid-structured chain of command, they all are lower performance compared to cooperative systemic organizations, from a Fortune firm to a local nail salon. You can feel the culture of competition or cooperation if you simply pay attention. This model of competitive thinking perpetuates, "That's the way we have always done it" thinking—the mark of a dying enterprise at the C-suite level. This is true in institutions, nations, education, and leading Fortune 10,000 firms. Their market share atrophies and they have no clue why. Yet they continue this "what they know" management versus "how to *grow*" management. The pyramid organization system is a failed model that stifles cooperation, creativity, solution dynamics, employee retention, client retention, customer service, institutional problem solving, and, finally, desired and required performance elevator outcomes. A wave of cultural reform in organizational theory is sweeping the world as new leaders value cooperative culture reform to increase performance. Investing in obsolete culture systems—failed competitive measurement and assessment tools—is fatal to brand leadership in any market. From dentist offices to Fortune institutions, there are ongoing cultural upgrades from competitive processes into *cooperative* processes.

Cooperative cultures foster:

- Accountability
- Recognition
- Reward
- Celebration

Competition is not always transparent and can operate in an opaque systemic model. Cooperation, though, is fully transparent and has no secrets outside next-generation releases of trade-secret IP. Competition critiques. Cooperation *plusses*. Competition depletes us and is toxic to our spirit. Cooperation replenishes us and is inspiring to our souls. Human nature thrives in cooperation and collaboration, as do institutions. Human nature is over-stressed and slowly dies in a competitive environment. Cooperation motivates. Competition resides in fear and threat. Competition is an error, a flaw in brain source code. This software bug is being removed from collective human consciousness. If you wish to fast-track your own growth in this area, I submit two bibles for personal development, national development for lawmakers and heads of state, administrations for individual leaders, from Fortune leadership to cigar shop owners (send me some cigars as a thank you). It is cooperative:

1. *Redemption: The Cooperation Revolution* by Berny Dohrmann
2. *Becoming Supernatural: How Common People are Doing the Uncommon* by Dr. Joe Dispenza

Becoming Supernatural is the leading brain software reprogramming book published by Hay House. I mentored my buddy, Louise, founder of Hay House Publishing, before, during, and to her last garden party into her graduation with honors in this work. Trust Joe's work—job well done, Joe. You were early in your pre-2020 work—a lighthouse for the SUPER CHANGE brain that cannot wait to upgrade its software into full magnificence in a one-two punch of reading. These two books read *you* from right where you are now, and when you are complete, you land where you always desired.

Bill Gladstone, founder of Waterside Productions, and I have been working for a lifetime to advance consciousness. When Bill read *Super Change* and *Digital Manners,* he said, "Please, it has to be Waterside." I said to this SUPER CHANGE team and brain—you bet.

Make a note of tools, tactics, things to do, follow-up reads, and alternative process skills acquisition to master and lead in SUPER CHANGE after your first read. This work is designed to engineer outcomes you cannot acquire outside the work itself—and unlike so many obligations to grow leadership, you hold the keys to the future in your hand; and the work is what you already knew anyway, and the outcomes are easy to download. As you share this work with circles, clients, suppliers and your teams, do so in gratitude. Gratitude is the mindset of Super Changers.

An increasing number of SUPER CHANGE C-suite managers are reforming cultures from competition to cooperation, using the step-by-step template contained in *Redemption: The Cooperation Revolution*, repeated in this work for a reason. *Redemption* has been back-ordered at Amazon since release in 2010 as a global change agency, and is a five-star-rated best seller; a book for tomorrow's leaders of state, Fortune leadership at all levels, institutions, and corner eyeglass fitters, as well as everywhere else. (Amazon fills your back-orders in seventy-two hours, usually). I would order ten for your best clients, as they will thank you for years for that gift-wrapped acknowledgement to your best accounts. It will inspire repeat buying, customer loyalty, and the immediate referral marketing you may be missing. Be a gift giver in SUPER CHANGE because acknowledgement sells.

Families are taxed the same way as institutions, so families also must adapt to SUPER CHANGE to thrive. Those who fail to thrive in SUPER CHANGE have family cultures that are miserable versus those that are on-fire, switched-on, and turned-on in everyday life. Competitive families are typically incomplete in every way, in all lifestyles. My switched-on, turned-on home life inspires leaders I mentor and is a consequence of working with each other as mother and father, and in working with our nine children and our large circles, which are all cooperative and cooperatively reinforcing. We are SUPER CHANGE embracers in both home and in work spaces, and we are excited about the shifts that are coming next as our greatest adventure in human experience is ever-unfolding. Our family values are like rungs on a ladder: rung #1 is our relationship with God; rung #2 is our relationship with each other as soulmates; rung #3 is our relationship together as parents to our adopted and natural children;

rung #4 is our relationship with balanced recreation and our planet; and rung #5 is our relationship with contribution and career.

The secret is that the space between these rungs represents our values, and they are by no means equally spaced. Our children know and now teach it to their children—if we cooperate and never re-order the rungs of our ladder, our lives will always *thrill us*. What does your ladder look like? Is this useful to reframe it? For singles, it is the same, but replace the relationship with your ideal goal, and then leave that outcome to God. For agnostics, read *Becoming Supernatural* by Joe Dispenza.

Future AI creations and adaptations, and genetically improved humans, are designed for SUPER CHANGE—they are programmed for it. Trans-humans may have more in common with AI than with wetware of bygone eras who fail entirely to adapt to SUPER CHANGE. Those obsolete and unteachable brains will die off sooner than you expect as we reside in forward SUPER CHANGE longevity together. Can you not feel the *great awakening* across the entire planet?

We, as wetware from the past, will either upgrade our software to embrace SUPER CHANGE, or we will wither and live miserable lives resigned from participation in the SUPER CHANGE age. We will be left behind and left out. Such humans will live in abject loneliness within SUPER CHANGE total connectivity. You see it now everywhere in the world: aligned, collaborating nations and excluded competing old model nations, aligned cultures and excluded cultures. Old Brains are killing each other. New Brains are expanding the global real estate of peace and security for one another and their unborn. System abuse is increasingly considered a virus, as insane competitive economics that can never be sustained. Cheat, join the competitive crisis in integrity for humans, and we harm life on the planet and our own lives. Self-correct with integrity, and we will thrive and add longevity to all life on the planet. Trans-immortal humans are Super Changing to a future that may include your own. Not only is our mental software ever more rapidly upgrading, but so is our hardware—AI Pacemakers, AI hearts, AI DNA-grown new organs with no rejections, new mechanical replacements for worn-out body parts—all coming to make us ever more trans-human, the next generation of human and AI partnership in our own evolution. Real AI is coming whether or not you are ready, and that AI will be a billion times smarter than me or we who mentor Fortune institutions. I am not being left behind. Keeping current is a lifestyle of mine. I mentor my client leaders to excel in SUPER CHANGE leadership priorities and outcomes. Send me the leaders of the world and I will send you back the SUPER CHANGE transformers of tomorrow. We are now in our fourth decade of press-ranked leadership outcomes in SUPER CHANGE. Your book on SUPER CHANGE is designed to mentor you when you lack the time or resources to engage me to do so. I hope you benefit individually and collectively as your leadership development is soaring.

Shareholders are seeking boards of directors who will hire SUPER CHANGE leadership. The old model is a hostile, competitive board with leadership engaged in endless conflict. A SUPER CHANGE board with an old model leadership—competitive modeling from obsolete university education with antique, out-of-age curricula and insane competitive leadership training—also exist in conflict. Acceleration and change are not taking place in such firms, and so they now wither and die as a desert of creative solutions takes form within their limited capacity to adapt into SUPER CHANGE accelerations. See Kodak, once dominant in film. See Circuit City (oh, I'm sorry, you can't). See the end of national bookstore brands (gone). See Sears, while you can, and try and find Toys "R" Us. Old, competitive, leadership and management have no future. Keep score. Now you know the *why* of it—buggy, competitive, retarding mental software. SUPER CHANGE is the cause.

The John Sculley board that fired Steve Jobs almost bankrupted Apple. Old Brain, old software, for brother John. Steve, whom I mentored, was a New Brain. Steve Jobs—with his new board model and management—forged one of the highest cap rate institutions in the world via accelerating SUPER CHANGE organizationally. The results were a reflection of the culture of creation, the new cooperative management model so resisted by the old board. The new board embraced Jobs and SUPER CHANGE, and created untold wealth and innovation for Apple shareholders. At the time of this publication, I am an Apple shareholder because New Brains rock it.

The crisis is, first and foremost, caused by a competitive mind virus of failed individual and collective integrity. In the old competitive, exploitive, failed, human organizing model, the following takes place:

- Chemical firms dump toxic waste in water supplies and landfills.
- Chemical firms dump toxic waste into sacks of food fertilizer.
- Volkswagen criminally engineers "cheat devices" for gas mileage and pollutes environments.
- Tobacco firms kill millions. All this occurs while not only knowing how harmful and addicting nicotine is, but through increasing its Bad Brains, engineering higher potency specifically to create greater, and more lethal, addiction. The highest cost to humanity is healthcare cost from these and other Old Brain pollutions of our planet and our bodies without consequence.
- Pharmaceutical companies lie about side effects and kill us. Baby Powder causes cancer and the jury said they knew. Insanity in brains making decisions in competitive models unreformed into SUPER CHANGE.
- Food manufacturers use expedient toxic ingredients in their products to maximize short-term profits. The health costs and societal problems this causes are insane.
- State leaderships around the world save money by using

cheaper water that shortens life because of but horrific side effects caused by lead.

- Banks we all trust create phony accounts, fix interest rates, and conduct criminal actions, stealing a trillion dollars and paying a small fine to get out of jail free. This competitive, insane, systemic leadership crime does pay, and it pays well. Eventually, such integrity bankruptcies reach the real world. Eventually, leaders find they are actually not too big to jail. I am waiting for it... are you?
- "Profits over humanity" mindsets define antique thought and pollute society and the planet for generations. This is virus-induced output that degrades cultures and nations into obsolescence in SUPER CHANGE.
- SUPER CHANGE Old Brains operate competitive capitalism. Their model is to maximize profits *monthly* (insane time frames) for shareholders *at any cost* to reach record profits.
- New Brains focus to obsession on improving the outcomes for their customers *while* making a profit through cooperative capitalist modeling—a new SUPER CHANGE economic theory.

New Brain AI capitalism is cooperative, and cooperative capitalism is replacing all forms of failing competitive economics, because it is simply *a far better way*. Cooperative capitalism will replace communism, socialism, and competitive capitalism. There are failed models, as we can all easily see, and they are based on unresolved and unnecessary human poverty.

Tip: Purchase from cooperative providers, and stop purchasing from competitive capitalistic companies. Speed up the future as a SUPER CHANGE buyer, individually and corporately. Cooperative, integrity-based capitalism restores the planet and us.

SUPER CHANGE leaders are social investors. They exist to better distribute social capital so that no nation and no individual is ever left behind again. SUPER CHANGE is all about advancing human experience by transforming the failed, corrupt models of communism, socialism, and competitive capitalism into the Cooperation Revolution—a better way forward for humanity. The economic culture, the fabric of global systems, will change. Integrity is central in SUPER CHANGE economics, but it is an impossible characteristic when set inside competitive laws that foster the elite over the many. The *few against the many* economics is the cause of all poverty, strife and wars. Economics drives everything. If politics drives economics, we end up with super crash and war every time. If economics drives politics, we have prosperity and growth, *every time*.

That is what we all pray for in our futures—a far better way. No individual, no nation, left behind. Can we do better? We can, and we are, and we must, or we will become extinct.

Just think about this concept for a bit.

I have spent my own life in contract work with heads of state to foster these cooperative SUPER CHANGE principles in their nations' agendas. I only work with nations and institutions at Fortune Grade that seek systemic-level cooperation culture reforms in their development. David Corbin is one of my partners in this work. Using his great publication, *Illuminate: Harnessing the Positive Power of Negative Thinking*, we search the world to find those specific kinds of truly inspired SUPER CHANGE leaders, and *we* serve them.

Education no longer teaches global civics, leadership, self-reliance, rule of law, or integrity. Since integrity is a defining aspect of thinking and of collective culture, today we see a global epidemic of integrity breakdown for individuals and institutions. We are now inside the great integrity crisis—the problem itself. Education's first job is to prepare its student bodies for the times in which they live. In an era devoid of financial literacy, ask yourself some SUPER CHANGE questions:

Why did education replace civics and rule of law—from K-12 through higher education—with courses to memorize old war dates?

In the Entrepreneur Age, why is education not preparing its students for the fact that over fifty percent of all employment is through self-employment? Why is there a lack of entrepreneur education when the work space wishes to hire entrepreneur-trained brains?

Why is structured, memory bot education (a feature of the 1800s Industrial Revolution) fostering useless mental skill sets for the unstructured digital world that students will face moving into their futures? We teach memorization, and we test and reward for memorizing. We do not reward free thinking, original thinking, creative thinking, or critical thinking. We punish all education that the students must acquire to be hired, and we reward all the memorization skills for which the workspace has zero use. The failure to retool education reform globally (as a G100 model for all humans), will prove to be the single most contributing factor toward human absolute extinction, if not resolved. Dumbing down eight billion brains leaves those at the bottom with software that is so damaged that those brains join ISIS, Taliban and other brands of equally insane brains. The press needs to label and rebrand all deviant horror in news and the world as, "*Crazy brains* acted out again today," instead of giving the insane brains any authority or credibility.

Stop asking why. Crazy brain "why" is uniform... they are nuts.

Why are irrelevant skills being taught to student super learners in an age in which God invented *search*?

Why are hugely relevant skills required of SUPER CHANGE age thinkers not being taught in public or private schools? You all know how education is not what it could be as a human elevator. Now understand the threat to our global futures if education is not reformed today in SUPER CHANGE. If we do not reform education, anticipate AI will, and soon.

In only twenty years, the one hundred billion dollars spent on home schooling demonstrates that SUPER CHANGE brains will out-think, out-pace, and replace antiquated institutions. Entrepreneur-leading charter schools, such as the Harmony Schools of Dallas, or SuperCamp, Bobbi DePorter's adventure into education in San Diego and her Youth Success Weeks serving public education, are leading on the bleeding edge.

Contact SuperCamp and ask about the Youth Success Weeks if you wish to become part of the cooperation reform agency sweeping the entire world. I advise the board of Youth Success Weeks with my fellow education reformers, Bobbi DePorter of San Diego and leader Stedman Graham of Chicago, both of whom are superstars of SUPER CHANGE.

Unstructured, individually paced education focuses on entrepreneurial master skills, and now all other classic skills exist only in support. Learners want to read and learn math because they can see the relevance to their dreams. Today's super learners drop out, self-educate, and start their own lives and futures. Unreformed education has become irrelevant. *New Brains need context to content.* Cooperative educational cultures are out-pacing old models of competitive educational cultures and leaving national planners in the dust—stuck on their buckboards—in a new SUPER CHANGE educational starship world.

No one wants the keys to the car when they can travel to their destination by beaming up, using warp drive and beaming back down. Antique thinkers in education ("That is the way we have competitively always done it") will be like old soldiers who soon fade away into oblivion without anyone even knowing their "why." *We* know, though. Their "why" is a mindless falling into, "Because that is the way we have always done it," mindset, coupled with a, "Not on my watch," to the SUPER CHANGE mentality. Boards need to be free of those toxic, Old Brain, educational mindsets. Instead, SUPER CHANGE boards will reward SUPER CHANGE innovation and culture reform. The bottom line never lies.

Click www.superteaching.org to see one technology we created with proofs for SUPER CHANGE learners. Blocked by my model in education:

1. If you want to graduate in politics, run for local office.
2. If you want to master in politics, run for state office.
3. If you want to double master in politics, run for national office.
4. If you wish a PhD in politics, run for any school board.
5. If you want multiple PhDs, serve on the board of any university or in Washington on the DOE

In my own PhD experience with education, those inside it know well that unless we globally reform education, we will become extinct. The problems we created can no longer be solved by the brain software that brought us those problems—we need upgraded education to download better software to our minds.

Education: A Crisis of Integrity – Failure in Culture

Education is funded by *the few against the many* mentality to perpetuate insanity in economics in order to consolidate wealth to the owners who control it all. Until we change *that*, we are slaves to the owners. I know the owners and I served as head of a public investment banking institution serving them. When I stopped serving them, they sent me to prison. I learned a lot about the owners. After thirty years inside the largest business community in the world, I seek to transform their thinking, with their permission, for a better way forward. Extinction seems insane.

Because integrity, as a thinking skill set, is not yet part of institutional education, there follows a crisis for integrity leadership worldwide. Value, culture and community, civics and rule of law, were part of education when I studied in the 1960s and 1970s, but then it was removed in the 1980s nationwide, all at once. Civics of how to be a great citizen was taken out. Did anyone ask why or protest in the streets? We educated wage slaves in the 1980s and 1990s. Major high schools graduate forty-eight percent of their students. How are we doing out there? Old Brain politicians wish to pay existing educators much more for doing nothing more. No reform.

We are turning out ever more miserable lower middle class wage slaves as we stopped the *many for the many* mentality and moved into the *few against the many*, institutionalizing that system where the public never had a clue at all. After all, it is your children and your grandchildren we are Super Changing next. We have great leaders and we have great managers. We also have an absolute crisis of integrity in all leadership and communities—personal integrity, family integrity, and community integrity. Political integrity? Forget about it.

> You can never resolve the integrity crisis of leadership in the world at every micro and macro level with antiquated thoughts, or with education that fails to teach culture values, starting with the integrity of its citizens.

> Integrity comes first as the frame that holds all new, upgraded, brain code in RAM as integrity must talk to all your other loaded and open programs at the same time.

The culture of integrity defines a thriving culture and a thriving leader with endless mobility. Leadership without integrity is failed leadership, individually and collectively. Competitive leadership cannot exist inside the box top rules of integrity. Competition is corrupt, and it is impossible to sustain a culture of integrity within a culture that is, at its core, entirely insane brain software. Competition is an insane impulse of mind. I hope not yours.

However, cooperative leadership (sanity) will only co-exist with integrity. Integrity is the DNA of the cooperative SUPER CHANGE revolution that is taking place today in the mind field in all nations.

How do you fix the epidemic entropy that causes breakdowns in modern organizations, like at a dentist's office with three staff members, or a Fortune firm with 140 divisions and 600,000 employees worldwide? First, identify the problem as a breakdown in *integrity,* which is both cultural and individual. Then, construct a model where developing a culture of integrity fosters trustworthy leadership.

Study Dr. David Gruder's book, *The New IQ: How Integrity Intelligence Serves You, Your Relationships, and Our World*, and David Corbin's book, *Illuminate: Harnessing the Positive Power of Negative Thinking.* The cooperation revolution is impossible without integrity, and I encourage leaders looking for mentorship to consider my team— Gruder, a top-ranked TED Talk and Keynote speaker, and David Corbin—mentors. I engage them and have used them for years myself. We work together on larger corporate culture reframes in annual vision planning retreats for SUPER CHANGE outcomes. Google the growing list of cooperative and integrity culture focused mentors in the market today. Lead and bleed by engaging your favorite flavor soon.

If I remain in integrity with you, you might cooperate with me. If you break your integrity with me, or I with you, we will tend to put up our shields—put them up *fully*—and come to expect future out-of-integrity, competitive, self-absorbed behavior. When we compete, no one expects integrity. Leadership—in a model based on distrustful negotiations—is inefficient and impaired. This competitive model of leadership is well on the way out.

For this reason, the education dropouts have forged their own SUPER CHANGE institutions. They have bypassed obsolete generational and global educational institutions that failed to adapt. Their net worth, customer bases, shareholder wealth, and happy lifestyles would be impossible with today's broken educational lag to keep pace with SUPER CHANGE. Steve Jobs with Apple, Mark Zuckerberg with Facebook, the founders of Google, WhatsApp, Pinterest, WeChat, VOX, GPS, Uber, Tesla, YouTube, and Microsoft... as their institutions and ventures surge into being ever-forward SUPER CHANGE institutions, all are works in progress with a cooperative culture organizational theory. They are not simply thriving *in spite* of misplaced classic education, their C-suites are forged on SUPER CHANGE. At least a million others like them are starting up in the USA every year. We name them "unicorns," a concept that did not exist in education a decade ago. Unicorns are solutions that bypass broken education without upgrading global reforms. Can we do better? We should and we must. The unborn we serve scream at us all on our watch. Yesterday is already too late. We have the resources. What we lack is the cooperation and the will that go with it!

The future is coming. New Brains are already ready for SUPER CHANGE—plan on *that*.

CHAPTER 4

ACTION

GOSH, CEO SPACE INTERNATIONAL IS now in its fourth decade! I founded CEO Space to lead a mind-bending C-suite upgrade process that could advance new, whole-brain mental software while accelerating relevance and modernity for leaders. Today, in 150 nations, CEO Space International has become the number one Forbes-ranked "you can't afford to miss it" business conference in the world, along with ever-growing press rankings from other publications. For ten years, third-party press have uniquely ranked CEO Space International as the one business conference that leaders from Fortune institutions, entrepreneurs, and professional CEOs cannot afford to miss. It is ranked number one in the world. Serving hundreds of thousands of CEOs who employ millions across the world, over thirty years (like the Farmers Insurance ad on television) has taught us a thing or two about CEO and leadership development into SUPER CHANGE. Our industry-leading programs appeal to individuals and institutions. Click to explore www.ceospace.net.

The ability to stay the number one press-ranked leadership "currency" option—the calm in the eye of the SUPER CHANGE cyclones roaring across all of our lives—remains precious, as does the CEO Space challenge to ever-improve leader development in our fourth decade. Those skills that no book can ever impart by itself occur in CEO communities that learn together via new solution practices, all of which are customized to each leader. Leaders inform us that they finally have the experience for which they have been searching—one worthy of their limited time blocks. Leaders change as they practice to determine what works for them and what does not fit.

While CEO Space International remains the press-ranked leading *process*—versus being simply an "event"—for upgrading CEOs and their teams into SUPER CHANGE, we have spawned many others like Greg Reid's *The Secret Knock,* which is sold out every single time, or the Habitude Warrior Camp, with my mentee and brother in the work, Erik Swanson. The Annual Marketers Cruise is in January. Join me and September and we will meet you on board. James Dentley of Chicago's advanced trainings; Adam Markel's speaker camps; Blink's world domination events, at which I speak; Sharon Lechter's Play Big Movement; any of Jack Canfield's or Bob Proctor's events; and Tony Robbins excels at any and all of his current experiences. We compare notes to help each other be better leaders. The Bug Life in Vegas is another bleeding edge new process for leadership in SUPER CHANGE. Check these out—just explore to find the culture that fits best, and they will lead to others. Good? Answer the question, *what is your process to become and remain current in the unfolding SUPER CHANGE?* For that *is* now. It is your very next priority as an inspired leader.

All my endorsed events foster mental software that embraces SUPER CHANGE and ensures leaders thrive in this new age of cooperation cultures and collaborative silo leadership. This commitment is a process that is an entirely new experience for managements and awake leaders seeking out advanced SUPER CHANGE success planning. Our CEO Space process remains unique in the market, as we alone offer another advanced leader invention of *lifetime memberships* so that CEOs can return on-demand and on their own schedules, five times every rolling twelve months, to stay synchronized with advancements in the SUPER CHANGE marketspace. This recalibration is available every sixty days to all of our leadership members. CEO Space remains the leading brand— one heralded repeatedly by third-party press ranking number one worldwide—and the leading value option to advance agile minds, into fully relevant, leading-edge principles of leadership inside the unfolding SUPER CHANGE age. The connections made at these conferences are of legendary proportions. CEO Space has not raised its price since 1988, another exclusive value unmatched by other offers. No other offer can match the prices of our lifetime memberships (individual or corporate), which include money-back warranties. When you compare programs, do several over time to find the best fit. Then, as a SUPER CHANGE leader, *learn, earn and return*.

Join cultures in leadership development where you contribute as much as you consume—cooperative cultures versus competitive.

No single program, not our own CEO Space or any other, can resolve all issues that face silo managers in all industries. Solutions must be customized over time, always with the leader's input. Leaders are challenged as never before to find time to de-stress and resolve challenges in a safe, proven, confidential environment. This is the ticket to your own World Series process for ongoing leadership development.

Adam Markel, legendary trainer of Peak Potentials Training, operates as that gig was retired by Richard Tan, CEO of Success Resources, the largest training firm in the world today. I was a keynote speaker at Peak Potentials from its start to its closing. I encourage our Peak family worldwide to explore the programs suggested here that appeal to you for ongoing development. Today, Adam operates the most advanced speaker development camp for leaders seeking to brand fertilize their markets, using speaking and publishing to celebrate their brand in more wide footings. Online resources magnify leaders who are also speakers. Adam's program, Heart Space, has created more successful speakers than any program we have monitored. I sent my wife, September Dohrmann, President of CEO Space, with her all-lady team and board leadership. This work led to her a standing ovation at the General Assembly of the United Nations and keynote talks across the world. Thank you, Adam, for a cooperation-based leadership development program for on-stage planet shifters. My wife and I thank you for your Peak years and your Heart Space speaker camps that followed. Your bestseller, *Pivot*, which was first released on CEO Space stages, is a hallmark read for all in SUPER CHANGE engaged in their own pivot today.

As you study available options to advance your own leadership development, check out the alliance and affiliate partners on the CEO Space web site www.ceospaceinternational.com. All those brands have been vetted on background complaints (zero) and proof that they *do what they say they do* by third-party firms retained by CEO Space. This due diligence is required of our entire faculty in order to mentor in our high-level, Fortune-grade space. All those reports, including those on my background, are vetted by CEO Space. The reports appear in www.cleardirectory.com. A small, one-time fee is charged for non-CEO Space members for unlimited access to Clear Directory.

CEO Space members reading SUPER CHANGE may always access Clear Directory, meaning the persons inside have been cleared by CEO Space for mentorship, integrity and trust. Third-party counter-intelligence services with past and current work for the NSA, CIA and others, including US Army intelligence work, have performed, on your behalf, due-diligence confirmations at the highest industry standard. Systems replace trust in cooperation modeling. Use background resources when you are ready with new currency in SUPER CHANGE, when ethics and integrity on such detail become your next priority. For leaders, may we suggest CEOs reward leaders with upgrade retreats to the specialized flavor you select for training that most fits your culture.

The tools and tactics throughout this book provide options to explore your own process and discover mentors to upgrade to your leadership skills and mind software. Making options that were invisible to your personal development and growth visible is a never-ending challenge of SUPER CHANGE. Our goal is to unfold growing menus of options you can explore at your leisure as the best fit for you. Remember, your current software has one feature—your mind, and your mind alone, will always make you right, even if you are wrong. Think about the value of development into SUPER CHANGE to be more right and less wrong, if that is important to you as an inspired leader.

Your investment in time and resources to upgrade leadership development, personal development, and the wetware of your thought processes to your internal circles, will position you to embrace and thrive in SUPER CHANGE. This is your new "next." Leadership's next priority unfolds the second that you have an inkling that SUPER CHANGE is being resisted in any way by you or your team's current state of thinking.

Examine your competition barometer. If you are comfortable with being the top shark in the marketplace feeding frenzy and wish to remain in that feeding frenzy as if it were good and socially beneficial, you are mildly insane. If you fail to upgrade your software, you will eventually become irrelevant. You will never keep your brand current in the SUPER CHANGE market with that buggy, competitive software code. Competition sucks as a method of system modeling to prosper inside SUPER CHANGE. Competitive thinking is a form of insanity, and contrary to university and higher education, insane asylums turning out one white shark after another. As a result, these institutions are becoming increasingly irrelevant. If education fails to retool its capacity to prepare its graduates for the thinking required to prosper in the marketplace following graduation, it becomes obsolete. To remain current, education must retool its internal culture, its leadership process of development, and its curriculums to acknowledge that competitive thought is a form of human insanity and is toxic to future outcomes for humanity. New SUPER CHANGE curriculums will model after advanced work from Harmony and other college preparatory schools that reformed and retooled their education models into SUPER

CHANGE purpose-driven entrepreneur education, which I encourage wealthy readers to fund. Fund leading revolutions like Harmony Charter Schools, for example, in all fifty states. Cease funding antique, out-of-touch, out-of-date institutions who are failing to turn out the leaders of tomorrow. That *is* the way they have always done it, and they are sticking to it.

Donate to Bobbi DePorter's SuperCamp for Success Weeks in education nationwide, with annual donations and endowments. Yesterday is already too late for that one hundred million dollar endowment from Gates and others to both organizations. Our unborn cannot pay the cost of our delay today.

Do you need to take action to upgrade your mental software as a leader? Ask yourself these questions:

Do you exist in a competitive or cooperative culture as defined by the book *Redemption: The Cooperation Revolution*? You will know as you read the book.

Do you exist in the highest integrity, or do you lie to yourself about your cultural model? Are your teams acting out of a SUPER CHANGE truth, where high integrity is praised, rewarded, and culturally esteemed? or is "white shark" exploitation in dog-eat-dog cultures rewarding those who eat road kill? You will know as you read *Redemption* if you have any remaining doubt from reading just this. Leaders *know* the truth.

Do you eat your own young, or raise them and mentor them in ethics and integrity? At ever-rising standards? Do you grow yourself as a goal versus a destination?

How do you assess and grow your personal integrity as part of a SUPER CHANGE process to which leaders are increasingly committed?

Who is your SUPER CHANGE mentor, or do you even have one? Every leader requires a SUPER CHANGE mentor. I seldom have slot openings, but you can check, and CEO Space has oceans of mentors on its faculty for any level of leader. You are not serious about upgrading into SUPER CHANGE unless you have an expert mentor in this topic who will help you. Tony Robbins is one of the best, but seldom with open bandwidth. We, who lead in this space, are hyper-engaged to serve you, the leaders of tomorrow. Do you have the best possible SUPER CHANGE mentor? I have mine, and I work with others at all five CEO Space events. My own growth is a sixty-day process, not an event.

The obligations of SUPER CHANGE leaders come in stages and priorities. First, a SUPER CHANGE leader wishes to reform their work and family cultures from competition to cooperation. *Redemption: The Cooperation Revolution* documents new IP processes for advanced leadership in achieving these objectives rapidly. The book is a workbook of step-by-step leadership outcomes for the switched-on, turned-on, often overlooked home space, as well as the local or international workspaces. It is the first blueprint for forward leader action.

Second, a SUPER CHANGE leader wishes to engage Integrity Coaches, as I have for years, such as Dr. David Gruder. They work with individuals on personal leadership integrity, which is a life-long and serious commitment. When I discover a critical partner or leader who is not investing in integrity management upgrading, I think, "Uh-oh! A missing process needs to be installed." This is an investment in syncing with SUPER CHANGE marketspaces that is both the first and next step, and one that must be continuously worked. Otherwise, your cultural changes will fall apart, or rapidly accelerate, depending upon your own personal integrity and the integrity of your teams. There *is* no loyalty without integrity. There is no honor or work ethic without both loyalty *and* integrity. There is no integrity destination. We all wear masks. We all lie. We lie to ourselves and we often do not know it at the time. Integrity coaching reduces your lying. I thought I was a great leader.

For a long period of years, I ran a publicly traded global investment banking firm. I was a chairman and the founder of CEO Space International. While working with world leaders, I thought that I was in *my* highest integrity. Boy was I wrong. When I worked with Dr. David Gruder, bestselling author, Fortune leadership integrity trainer, award-winning TED Talk speaker, author of *The New IQ: How Integrity Intelligence Serves You, Your Relationships, and Our World*, I thought, "Well, I'm almost there." But, five years later, "almost there" is never actually a destination. *Integrity is a journey you travel for the remainder of your life.* You grow and learn and get better. You also "see" with new eyes real integrity and the lack of integrity everywhere.

After five years of the hardest, most intense, personal leadership development of my life—and I've been mentored by Tony Robbins, as well as the best-of-the-best like Napoleon Hill, Walt Disney, David Rockefeller and others at the top—I think... I am *in* the highest integrity there is. Then, as Dr. Gruder refits my self-assessment glasses from self-deception to 20/20 vision, like the song, "I can see clearly NOW."

Your definition of integrity changes. You become better, and your soul has new appetites so that plenty of integrity is never enough. You want *more*. Self-development for leadership skill is hard work, it is a process not an event, and it defines you as a leader if you commit to it. If your ego has you at the top of the food chain in income and bonus, what comes next is an adventure into your finest personal growth pathology in advanced leadership integrity. Your humility massively returns. Pick the mentor that is right for you, and dive into the work. If anything, my mentorship is respected because I *do* what I tell my leaders to do, and I did it first before I wake them up to what works. I know my leaders will win, because I already won. So many mentors tell you to do what they themselves have zero experience with. They are not *my* mentors. They did not do the work that they are teaching.

Third, a SUPER CHANGE leader commits to a process of upgrading year-to-year leadership core skills to prosper in the new age of SUPER CHANGE. Your decision-making strategies will keep you current inside the whirling global riptides of SUPER CHANGE once you adopt your own process for remaining current. The new "goalpost" for leadership is your process to remain current in the new age of SUPER CHANGE. New tools and new tactics are required and they are easy to acquire consistently in the *shift challenge* taking place for all of us who lead. From trade wars to real wars, third-party events affect the market place as never before. You must *pro*-act versus *re*act to these events without pausing. CEO Space is a model of a serious culture for leaders—from millionaires and billionaires to those in early development stages—where every leader in our community wishes to *become* current and *remain* current inside SUPER CHANGE. One hundred percent of CEO Space's 150-nation community is committed to the principles of cooperative leadership and cooperative cultures for any entity, from a nation to a home-based business.

My vision "saw" that by upgrading software for leaders of Fortune institutions to local small business, we would, over decades, not only improve their world, we would help improve *the* world. Today, ranked number one for a decade, I have great pride in the ever-improving, always current, CEO Space. Over thirty years later, third-party global press still state-ranked us number one worldwide. We are leading the entire industry of SUPER CHANGE, perhaps because we were also first. This also bred a top Forbes keynote speaker ranking for me, as well as a busy life, where last year I spoke worldwide, from the Gulf to India to Romania to the UK. This helps me assess what *is* going on out there in SUPER CHANGE all over the world. I love keynoting, and I invite all my readers to explore having me speak at your future events. Call Ellen Morgan anytime (256-850-4715) at the phone number that has never changed in almost half a century now. My talks on SUPER CHANGE inspire leaders in every industry.

I feature my own work with CEO Space as a SUPER CHANGE university program, which has spawned new institutions from our mentor graduates all over the world. We have featured some of these programs in this book for your exploration. Each culture-customized program was born in CEO Space for various markets where we continue to turn out fresh new offers in leadership development programs. Not only we providers *not competitive*, we *recommend* and *endorse* one another.

I wish to acknowledge that I resigned from CEO Space management in 2014. Since that time, our press ranking has been achieved by September, President, owner and CEO. September has massively upgraded our offers every year. As CEO, September has put in place all-lady leader teams, lady super boards, and demonstrated women at the top keep a SUPER CHANGE excellence I feel old-boy networks can never achieve. Again, leading in this space by *doing it*, by walking that talk. After all these years of global number one ranking, I wish to acknowledge the future generation of leadership that now tools CEO Space into 150 nations. These nations are now acquiring CEO Space for rapid, in-nation entrepreneur development. Leaders following this context of SUPER CHANGE may explore stepping back to actually reach impossible destinations by allowing others to take up the lead. I did it, and I often suggest that other leaders take this uncommon step into the better future. I encourage all leaders to ensure lady leaders are full partners on your boards and your leadership communities.

Competition is the sole virus of human thought that pollutes everything. Competitive thought impulse is the source of all human misery. Competition is the largest bug in human mental software, but, thankfully, it is the one master virus of the brain we can remove entirely. Removal is a choice made out of virus awareness. Once you grasp that principle, SUPER CHANGE becomes an adaptation you can model into effortlessly.

You can never remove a virus in your brain if you fail to know you are infected with a toxic mental virus—competitive thought impulse.

If you pause, procrastinate, or delay, you will squander your life instead of addressing your own virus removal opportunity. Time is your most important asset to move into cooperative, collaborative, supportive, nurturing, human problem solving, without competitive toxic derailing. To upgrade and embrace SUPER CHANGE (remember, you cannot get out of the SUPER CHANGE age) you need to realize, as I have suggested, you must simply calm down to catch up. Action is required to improve whole-brain software by reading, live training, YouTube video training, live mentors one-on-one, and keeping with your own process to remain current.

Choose your form of processing (action) that best helps you become current in SUPER CHANGE. Fully commit to staying current, which is how you and your community prosper. You might make a "Things To Do" list from this and other chapters. Review your mentor-suggested process list, then prioritize what comes first, second, and third for you and your teams.

Being and remaining current is a team sport. Re-invent your circle to buy into the principles of SUPER CHANGE and gift them copies of this book to harmonize your circles. Keep an inventory of *Super Change* on your bookshelf, and frequently, as a new process, gift *Super Change* to critical team, allies, customers and critical suppliers. You align your team as you do so.

Now, consider your community circles; who are those who are negative and competitive, and when do you remove them from your culture? The answer the first instant the thought crosses your mind. Bad brains are a toxic pollution in your workspace. Clean house the first time you become aware of your own toxic environment. Leaders clean house.

Elevating energy culture and moral integrity in your circles is a blessing of SUPER CHANGE leadership. Performance soars. Those released are not a culture fit moving forward. Use the book *Super Change* to discover who resists SUPER CHANGE in negative loops, and who embraces SUPER CHANGE moving forward. Insist on nothing less than unconditional support in your culture upgrade. I am amazed at purpose partners who are well paid, and then, in exchange for second of fame, trash the brand to the press while being paid. Create employment contracts with zero tolerance for brand-diminishing behavior without regard for cause. A culture of brand protection is a culture integrity leaders and AI will increasingly out as competitive Old Brain insanity. Trash the brand that pays you? It is insane for you and everyone else. Shareholders are not amused by a lack of integrity in a culture where cooperation has full accountability as systems replace trust by agreement in writing. Culture is defined by leadership box top rules.

Breakdown in integrity is an epidemic as failed competitive system models are breeder reactors for switched-off toxic workspaces defined by endless meetings that go nowhere. You will know them by their (as with all virus code) toxic secretions into your workspace. Are you awake enough to assess your own? To move if unhealthy or toxic? Today, moving is ideal as the work options are greater than the talent to fill them. Now is the time to exchange toxic competitive workspaces for cooperative switched-on, turned-on work spaces.

If they are not teachable, they are removed without blame or judgment. They thrive in toxic, highly competitive, malfunctioning organizations. Assist them to find one with the highest recommendation and severance package you can provide. All competitive, toxic workspace brains are dying inside SUPER CHANGE, which is reforming all workspaces today.

Your SUPER CHANGE adaptation is as strong, or as weak, as your own weakest link. Those relationships inside your choices for your own core circles into which you invest your life—your real wealth. Only tolerate quality in thinking and always upgrade thinking. Surround yourself with protected thought leaders who thrive in SUPER CHANGE, who live the learn-unlearn-relearn model, who adapt to SUPER CHANGE as a priority of their mental state—a higher state of leadership thinking that they choose and can control entirely. Those who fail to embrace, or even resist, these SUPER CHANGE principles should be replaced with improved-thinking, higher quality leaders in your core circles. You must seriously guard your leadership community, and then you must install a system to guard the guards.

Competition—a virus which can dumb down all of your progress—has a way of creeping back into places where it has been eradicated, until the collective human consciousness deletes competitive thought entirely. Imagine a world of one hundred billion humans in which we are all unconditionally collaborative and cooperative, supporting and nurturing, and where competitive thought is not possible. Would that be more like heaven? If competitive communities appear more like hell to you—why make hell your home or your workspace?

The brain's competitive thought impulse from the reptilian midbrain will bring all its high drama as competitive leaders know so well. Betrayals, divisions, endless gossip, blame drains, backbiting, and core wheel wobble, rob us of performance. This is impossible in more "managed systems." This is true for a car repair shop or a Fortune institution. The more smoothly operating system has less competition and more cooperation integrated into their culture in that higher functioning workspace. This duality exists because integrity is culturally depreciated or unappreciated as systems swing from competition into cooperation cultures. As you reform your home and work spaces, invest in integrity and cooperative culture building.

Leaders of tomorrow understand that cooperative culture building is the future for all brands, and your brand is the culture—your customer community knows if you understand this truth, and they feel it *instantly* if you do not. They reward cooperation, and consumers, as well as B2B, punish competitive relationships increasingly. Competition is dying as a model for organizing humans. Your customer service instantly tells us if you are competitive or cooperative. We can feel the difference, and the difference is enormous.

In the spring of 2019, following a horrible climate change winter globally, the USA led the world with 3.2% GNP growth. More importantly, productivity in America soared to a record output. This made inflation fall and values rise in all markets. This is impossible inside competitive cultures. The reformation of culture is demonstrating breakthroughs in performance and productivity. *There is an absolute ceiling on performance gains in competitive pyramidal structures.* SUPER CHANGE has altered the landscape of America and all global industry.

Leaders of nations might wish to regard that the corruption you so badly wish to downscale is endemic in competitive government cultures. Until culture is reformed to cooperative management at a national level, the epidemic of corruption will remain higher than desired. I work with progressive national leaders who are examining the AI blueprints for the easy reform of competitive cultures into cooperative cultures in their state stakeholder teams, which always works over time to limit the growth of corruption. Why?

Cooperation is a DNA forged on integrity. Will you continue to cooperate with me if I breach integrity with you? Cooperation requires higher ethics and integrity than competitive brains require. Competition requires almost no ethics and integrity. Those who reside in cultures of competition adhere to the belief—a Fake News

11th Commandment—*"Thou shalt screw unto others before thou are screwed unto."* This model of brain software is dying, yet remains a virus on human consciousness. Let's not perpetuate that lower level of Old Brain thought.

Act with consistent integrity, and your community will feel that cooperative value rising almost instantly. Assessing SUPER CHANGE cooperative culture quality and integrity as the DNA you always improve defines the winners in the new age of SUPER CHANGE. Is that winner going to include... *you*?

CHAPTER 5

THE EXCITEMENT AND LIMITATIONS OF SUPER CHANGE

THERE ARE LIMITATIONS IN SUPER CHANGE. The first is your wetware brain. You have not evolved for SUPER CHANGE, though you created SUPER CHANGE. The great conundrum of our time.

I know that first precept of SUPER CHANGE appears to be an oxymoron, but all of us wetware brains know this truth exists. We know evolution is super changing everything, including *us*, and this accelerated pace of change leads to future unknowns. This scares us because old wetware brains want to be safe and feel comfortable when challenged with the unknown, even when the unknown is exciting and unavoidable.

Today, we SUPER CHANGE with CRISPR, and AI CRISPR is coming next—millions of years of evolution can occur in a thousand seconds. We change corn and wheat. We change viruses and bacteria. We change cancer bullet cells and virus delivery CRISPR created. We change all life coming up next. Evolution is now in SUPER CHANGE due to AI moving beyond wetware control. Today, we are DNA-changing humans. Today, we are creating nearly immortal super humans, or *trans-humans* to whom we are the last of a species. We call such humans "entrenched wetware," or brains that resist SUPER CHAGE. These brains are mortal and die in short lifespans. Trans-humans, with consciousness backed up in real-time by AI, are immortal until they choose to exit wetware in favor of spiritware and go *next*. A decision. The SUPER CHANGE wetware are partners with AI collaborators, and that world is defined by the soon-to-be movie and best-selling 2020 book *Digital Manners* to follow as sequel to SUPER CHANGE. The fun read in which this leader development work provides tools and tactics for the new software your brain is now acquiring.

Your decision: *are you e-wetware or super change wetware?* As this book has changed your mind's software, you can never go back to not knowing your answer. Be at peace with your answer. You cannot stop the future of all SUPER CHANGE wetware. Either join them or pass in peace with communities of e-ware enjoying the last of that human Old Brain journey.

For the first time, we can engineer a head of lettuce or an ear of corn to a standard that farmers have been striving to reach for thousands of years. It is hardier, more water efficient, more insect resistant, more disease resistant. It delivers more yield per acre. More nourishment per pound. It has all of the good stuff Mother Nature would serve up after one hundred million years of her own forward evolution. Irrigated with engineered Super Water (www.superwaterhyox.com), producers enjoy Jurassic Park acre-yield improvement, without cost for pesticides or fertilizers, and save two thirds of water.

The crop taste, size and yield per acre breaks records with SUPER CHANGE water, but not really. Super Water is showing miracle health effects in the body. We are now serving it in SUPER CHANGE in one hundred *months* versus one hundred million *years*. My buddy, Tony Robbins, is involved in beef made without a cow. The best beef or chicken you ever tasted, always top grade, and no pollution from animal stocks or cruelty to animals. This new form of protein promises unlimited, healthier, nourishment for those who require it. This new technology promises a wipeout of the largest CO2 producer on Earth—cattle. The new nourishment removes toxic beef, which has chemical cocktails too complex for labs to track due to the ever-declining quality of mass production. From livestock to squash, we are *evolving*—not just changing—in the new age of SUPER CHANGE.

We modify water into Super Water, at a molecular level, with three times the oxygen we once had upon the Earth, where our ice cores from bygone ages show us how healthy water was. Now, in SUPER CHANGE, Super Water has returned again in 2020 to serve us via technologies that did not exist five years ago. Now, with SUPER WATER, we see crops that use fifty percent less water, no longer require pesticides or toxic fertilizers, and present Jurassic Park yields in agriculture one must see to truly believe. Check out www.superwaterhyox.com, a technology of SUPER CHANGE now transforming food crops worldwide. Having seen, I am a believer.

But wait—Super Water is a byproduct of the lowest cost unit of energy, extracted from water, with less energy in, and more energy out, with zero pollution. The final energy is not lithium—batteries polluting land by the millions—that only replaces an oil problem for a waste battery problem. No. The solution is the lowest BTU and kilowatt energy unit: hydrogen taken from water anywhere on Earth. Hydrogen is the future energy for planes, trains, ships, trucks and all transportation, and provides endless power generation at the lowest cost and environmental impact, resulting in self-sustaining, fully renewable energy. Super Water is the *byproduct* of the completed hydrogen energy breakthrough technology that will change the world. SUPER CHANGE unlimited cheap energy (and water cleanup and soil cleanup at the lowest cost ever known to date), all in one new trillion dollar cap rate institution as a *unicorn*, a SUPER CHANGE game changer.

We are doing the same in material sciences, from nano sciences to composites, as well as medical sciences, from CRISPR to AI CRISPR, to Dr. Jean Pierre's advanced bio research labs bringing us the trans-humans of tomorrow faster than you could anticipate. We are doing the same in software until the software is smarter than we are and writes its own code beyond anything we could understand or imagine. New life. We are creating new life with software that needs another name. We are creating living neural network brains today. Is your brain not a fleshy and chemical storage device for quantum whole-brain computing with self-evolving better software over your lifetime? Humans have created a future generation of new quantum field life. In SUPER CHANGE, we have no clue if this new life will serve us or see humans as a threat. In cooperation, such thinking cannot occur. In competition, flaws in our thinking and new life design may always occur. If competition is insane, do we labor to weaponize new life for military applications resulting in nations competing with each other using this new life weaponry? How will that new life think, act, and see us in the end? We do not know.

The Jurassic Park primary mantra—*life will always find a way*—is spooky to new AI life evolving without box top rules for culture and outcomes from nations of the world. Is it all a bit insane to you? Can we do better? Should we? Will we? When? Are you involved or a spectator, watching as a sidelined, uninvolved critic of your own real-life movie?

Globally, some legal and some illegal engineering is being conducted at the DNA level on humans, as well as for plants and animals. We are being engineered into super beings. Super brains. Super bodies. We are being engineered to be disease resistant, have longer lives, be more highly functioning, and far smarter. These new humans are *designed* to embrace SUPER CHANGE, while those with old-style wetware brains do not so easily adapt. We are engineering body part replacement. We are engineering robotic body part replacements as we move into real-time backup of your consciousness, the software that makes you, *you*. Elon Musk and others are working on that component of SUPER CHANGE.

First, inducing educational experience directly into your brain; second, backing up your real-time consciousness. Elon Musk launched the SUPER CHANGE to move from toxic petroleum products into alternative models for electricity and for transportation, sparking a five-year revolution in industry. SUPER CHANGE is exploding all around you and worldwide.

What privacy protections will exist in an everything-is-hacked world if your consciousness is resigning the real you of you on server firms updated in real time to every word you're reading in this sentence? What if your consciousness is hacked? Is anyone thinking these new box top rules through, or is SUPER CHANGE out of control?

We have to fight the impulse to resist SUPER CHANGE and instead re-learn how to *embrace* it as humans. New trans-humans thrive in SUPER CHANGE, where Old Brains may or may not. New humans view those with the inclination to repulse SUPER CHANGE as being a threat, when we are the threat to SUPER CHANGE, which remains unstoppable.

Upgraded brain software defines old, buggy, brain software (yours, perhaps) as both defective and limited. Competitive thinkers are seen by SUPER CHANGE brains as wholly insane in thought process and outcomes that repeat in endless loops of unwanted over-stress and tensions to desired outcomes. Because, folks, those who resist SUPER CHANGE are inferior embodiments of antique thought modeling that is dying out of humanity because it is a software of the mind that no longer supports human accelerations in natural evolution. The world is not flat, so do not malign me if I state unequivocally the Earth is a sphere and not at the center of a solar system where everything revolves around it. Do not put me in prison for my progressive future beliefs about tomorrow.

In generations to come, folks with Old Brains might be relocated to quaint developments that preserve old thinking. Villages that are dropping out to preserve Old Brain culture are here today worldwide.

The Amish are an example, but many Amish embrace SUPER CHANGE while preserving old traditions.

It may unfold far sooner than you think. Islands of Old Brain software, resistant to SUPER CHANGE, may become much like a zoo where SUPER CHANGE humans come to view Old Brains and their entrenched, antique cultures. Will SUPER CHANGE humans wonder how those Old Brains managed to spawn *them* and all the super-evolving AI in the first place?

They will be joined by AI robots and machines so advanced our imaginations and *Star Wars* films will all fall short. No movie has it down sufficiently. My new book, entitled *Digital Manners*, like the space films we all know so well, provides insight into one possible future. Watch for the sequel to *Super Change*, coming to you soon. A movie is in the works for *Digital Manners*. Personally, I believe it is a game changer in our own thinking. Get some popcorn, it's coming.

The AI of tomorrow will be far beyond the wetware of even the 2020 SUPER CHANGE decade. I welcome them all as the new normal. They, the future trans-humans evolving now, are the future of our species that will discover the stars, clean up the environment, preserve the Earth from extinction, remove aging and pandemics from the human condition, populate the universe with the best of the diverse cultures on Earth, and safeguard human longevity.

These SUPER CHANGE intelligences will cease all murders—both individual and caused by war—that happen because of the way we think. Murder, at any level, is proof of the insane software in our present wetware. Why are we killing each other in wars? Because of the way we worship God or do economics? Why are we competing as a threat to each other in the same species? Why are we competing until death, perpetuating a tradition of insanity? All forms of destructive competition reflect a form of human insanity—buggy brain software we can and must upgrade within ourselves. Why are we not cooperating? *That* is a display of our mental sanity and expresses far-improved human brain software... does it not? The Gulf punishment of religious diversity (over two thousand years of slaughter for the master faith idea), is an insane thinking model over which way you worship the same Allah—really? Are you kidding me? I've studied the Koran for four decades. There is no authority for death and mayhem in those pages. In today's time, less than ten percent of Muslims trash the moderations of ninety percent of faithful Muslims who hate all the death and violence. They consider it a form of ignorance. We all watch the madness over dinner together.

In any nation, call it what it is—insane. Insane thinking. How is it that the one virus—competitive thinking, a pure mental virus on human consciousness, a form of insanity—is such that we humans *continue* to perpetuate and protect and reward insane competitive thinking rather than reward and recognize sanely working to eradicate competitive thinking in our cultures entirely? Watching innocent human lives on prime time at dinner where the innocent is beheaded while we enjoy a warm meal. How is all that not insane when seen more objectively? The cause? Bad mental software requiring upgrading.

All human diversity will be celebrated in SUPER CHANGE as being precious. No human diversity will be punished as we evolve together under principles of cooperation and accountability. SUPER CHANGE will remove competitive thought from human existence as we evolve. *Sanity will win over insanity.* The antique thought forms of our human past are already imprisoned in firewalls of obsolescence. They have freeze-framed their current existence and drift through insignificant lives into a repeating oblivion of pain and suffering.

You must fight back against any impulse to stay with the status quo. Find your own way to read, remain current, and upgrade your evolving whole-brain software to live a life of *significant contribution* to the unfolding SUPER CHANGE age.

One software upgrade is one in which your now-more-awake brain sees SUPER CHANGE as a higher state of energy open to new software downloads from SUPER CHANGE itself. For your far-more-awake brain, the adventure of adapting and remaining current to each New Brain download is a worthy challenge of personal advancement and growth. Organizational progress into higher collaborative elevating performance standards is the new social capital toward which workplaces are striving. The cornerstone question for leaders today is, "What is *your process* to remain current in SUPER CHANGE?" If you lack a process, this book places you on a success path to develop your own process in SUPER CHANGE. We recommend options you can select, and they all lead to even more process options.

Yesterday is already too late for your process to commence.

New Brain culture flows down and outward into any organization, refreshing the paradigm, and refreshing the process system-wide. Old Brain culture flows upward (I will report you), and tends to block, retard, and derail performance improvements. It resists improvement because improvement is change, and Old Brains believe that change must be avoided at all cost. Old Brains incorrectly assess change as a threat to the way things are.

New systems in your home life and your workspace require recognition models that reward and acknowledge SUPER CHANGE adaptation. Embracing SUPER CHANGE must be rewarded in leading cultures to perpetuate SUPER CHANGE mental agility across the entire space of your culture. This process is self-correcting as it unfolds over time in culture.

A New Brain adapts so that all change is seen as welcomed improvement and cannot happen fast enough! How do you see your team? Have you developed a high-performance SUPER CHANGE team? Teams that welcome change as improvement? Teams with old software resist change and improvement, and they work to keep culture impoverished by guarding the Old Brain software model, "That is the way we have always done things." The resulting measurements are defined by the care we put into managing both Old and New Brains. The limitation of SUPER CHANGE is the seawall of Old Brains seeking to keep the organization "safe" from improvement, so that changes or upgrades to culture and mental software are stalled. The expanding New Brain organization still progresses exponentially and ever-renewably into its systems' innovations and never-ending quests for the highest expressions of excellence. SUPER CHANGE is now completely unstoppable. Unless leaders embrace a core process to continuously improve New Brain SUPER CHANGE software, their labors will ultimately fail in the market place.

Perhaps the most burning question is: will SUPER CHANGE futures include human beings at all, or will they proceed even more rapidly following our own pending extinction? Our continued survival as humans depends on our next evolution of mental horsepower. We must accelerate lifelong learning, unlearning, and, most importantly, relearning with mental software that embraces these new SUPER CHANGE mental tools. We must celebrate all human diversity and cease Old Brain insanity of punishing it. Look where that has gotten us.

Brand space that was once set in stone and considered sacred, must be renewed and reinvented quarterly in a SUPER CHANGE market space. Brands in SUPER CHANGE must be made relevant consistently to the highest customer outcomes, which is new for brand education as a whole. Consumers require ever-rising value in their evolving relationship with brands. Gone are the days we were brand loyal to Mother Goose or Tide. Icons like the Marlborough Man created brand loyalty. Could the Aunt Jemima brand launch successfully today? Brands like Campbell's Soup are transforming their brand modeling, as they all must to remain relevant.

It remains critical to provide fresh innovations to your customer base in never-ending brand renewals through ever-improved customer value. Shared experience itself is a SUPER CHANGE. Slowly, tomorrow's leading institutions are embracing SUPER CHANGE as curriculum—a massive, historic, seismic, new teaching event in education for us, and for the future of humanity.

This new thinking on brand relevance includes packaging, consumer quality upgrades, experience improvements, and customer service. Over time, these deliver pre- and post-sale experiences, plus eternal service improvements. It requires integrating quarterly, bi-annual, and yearly innovations into the organization's common annual master vision planning. Collective common vision drives brand renewals. Increasingly driven by social investing, the non-toxic and "life friendly" outcomes for brands has become a new essential. This ensures brand updating and sustainability in any space. In essence, new processes must continuously be initiated in order to retain brand relevance in the rapidly evolving marketplace in the new age of SUPER CHANGE. Who is taking that step for the solo entrepreneur or for the Fortune 100 institution today? Identify leading processes to become current and to remain current. We are losing our core capacity to adapt to SUPER CHANGE... which we now see everywhere.

In SUPER CHANGE, the current, leading, management processes are defined at annual retreats to *reset leadership* to the always-new, common, enterprise vision for the coming year. Vision renewal is the energy of empowerment for year-to-year corporate goal attainment. The organizational wheel then revolves around quality in the transmission of that common vision to the entire stakeholder base. Vision retreats define SUPER CHANGE leadership. Assess the quality and strategy in your workspace and whether you host annual vision retreats and release annual renewals of your brand via common vision from such retreats. Do you have them?

Install missing processes if you lack a proven, bleeding edge process to remain current in rapidly accelerating SUPER CHANGE. What is your process today? We keep asking for a good reason.

For larger institutions, Jeff Magee and I forged a forward institutional "common vision" renewal retreat pathology for Fortune institutions, with source management leaders of Fortune firms wishing to lead in

SUPER CHANGE engaging us. We then help those selected teams coordinate in system-wide, worldwide, family participation nights in which all stakeholders, suppliers, and contractor groups join virtual conferences to rally morale, cement the common vision as culture, and request non-negotiable, unconditional support. Recognitions reignite the community to higher performance in the subsequent 180 days between EPNs (employee participation nights). Those who create organizational "wheel wobble" are either developed in their human potential by upgrading their wetware mental software, or are exited and deleted from the community. SUPER CHANGE cultures hold culture accountable within a zero tolerance for organizational wheel wobbling. Zero tolerance raises the bar on your culture. It represents an entirely new aspect of New Brain leadership.

New Brain thinking is infectious and renews energy throughout the entire system so that recognition for individual contribution becomes far more important than market rate compensation. Installing cooperative recognition programs also pushes authority down and out from your new SUPER CHANGE all-hub management, into all outer wagon wheel spokes of divisions for unmatched growing momentum outcomes inside switched-on, turned-on workspaces. Old Brain leadership in organizations moves authority downward from pyramidal Old Brain software, perpetuating obsolete institutions run by competitive modeling based upon fear, punishment, and exploitation. This represents a dying brand space.

New Brains will leave Old Brain workspaces because, unlike Old Brains, when they see their contributions have no outlet from insane, Old Brain systems, they are gone at their lunch break and with no notice. Competitive systems can no longer retain talent. New Brains leave for more aligned cooperative cultures and institutions. Switched-on, turned-on workspace. Is that yours? Social careers mark the New Brain hire and turned-on, switched-on career paths versus stagnated jobs without relevance or context to work output—or context to anything. Creating value from the mailroom to the Chairman's office creates switched-on, turned-on workspaces of the future.

Leaders who know the difference are replacing leaders who do not.

For example, Family Participation Nights (a CEO Space Invention for leading managers) give formal recognition of the various sacrifices stakeholder families make over years of time. Family Participation Nights are low cost and infrequent (bi-annual is ideal), but help build a community of devotion that feeds institutional excellence. Accountability revolves around this celebration instead of the fear, punishment (you are warned, and then fired) and exploitation in a competitive organizational model. Every reader already knows that when any such family recognition lacks integrity, it's an experience that is a kind of soul death caused by the failed language of the obsolete system. Individuals are surprised and recognized across all silos in front of all peers via broadcast of Family Participation Nights, or FPN events (EPN—employee participation nights—are the same thing) which twice a year secure, as the new binding glue, SUPER CHANGE cultures solidly into place. Employee Participation Nights make the workspace culture relevant in both personal life and in work life. Institutions lacking this dynamic of essential SUPER CHANGE context present brands to the market that lack a connection to customers seeking higher social values from brands.

Those competitive cultures will die (have died, are dying) unless they are retooled at the systemic level. Performance in the competitive model has absolute ceilings on performance output. Whereas, in the book *Redemption: The Cooperation Revolution,* there is finally a full blueprint for leadership of an ideal cooperative system, and step-by-step tactics for Super Teaching culture reform at home and at work. *Redemption* is a leader's fully upgraded GPS for the New Brain leader seeking to learn "the how" tools to rapidly advance performance results in a SUPER CHANGE marketspace. Sears and Toys "R" Us management failed to read the book *Redemption,* and therefore resisted SUPER CHANGE until SUPER CHANGE left antique brands in the dust. Are you going the way of Sears, Kodak, Montgomery Ward, Pan American Airlines, Circuit City or Toys "R" Us? or are you moving the way of Tesla, Bezos in space, and Walmart with upgraded home delivery? Are you Uber, or driving a cab? Who has the better life?

SUPER CHANGE *requires* acceleration at all levels of human existence, from family and faith, to work and recreation. Think about all of it. You lead or you bleed, depending upon your embracement of or resistance to SUPER CHANGE. *Knowing* is half the battle, then decision-making follows. SUPER CHANAGE cultures define the future. Think about observing brains with old software or new, and *decide* to upgrade your own via a process you select. Nothing wonderful happens until a leader makes a decision.

We now have to calm down to catch up. We must be far more objective than we were prior to the new age of SUPER CHANGE. We have to invest in new processes to be brought current today, and then to remain current to prosper fully in the new future age OF SUPER CHANGE space. Next month, not next year. This is achieved by setting up your own personal mindset first, and your process and mentors second. First, you have to *know* you reside in an entirely new human age of SUPER CHANGE. Deny that, and you will lose relevance in your life value. Next, adopt and embrace the mindset that being current and remaining current is a great human growth adventure. Give up natural discomfort into change, where improvement becomes the excitement of the hunt. Shift all change to mean improvement. Improvement is not a threat to your midbrain. Your midbrain sees all change as a threat to be avoided because you might be eaten by those who no longer reside upon the Earth. The midbrain is looped and cannot unloop.

Stress is not a feature of SUPER CHANGE. *Stress is a feature of mental resistance to SUPER CHANGE.* You must adapt a stress-reduced lifestyle or be entrenched inside SUPER CHANGE. SUPER CHANGE resistance, with its enormous stress syndrome, is the new normal life for billions of humans today because no one taught us how to do better. Begin to see the world through new glasses. Choose to be a New Brain rather than an Old Brain. You alone control your own brain software. No one else. Not your mate. Not your circle. Just you. Be true to yourself.

As you gain ever-greater discernment, protect your developing circle of New Brain associations to rally around *you* and support you day to day, both in your home space and workspace. Spend far less time with Old Brains and assure your upgraded New Brain knows that difference as a leader in the workspace of the future. You cannot educate Old Brains — they are not teachable. Additionally, *you* are not *their* teacher. Keep those two ideas in mind and you will save a great deal of new balance and, of course, life energy. Are they teachable? Are *you* their teacher? Do not cast your pearls before swine who are deaf and dumb and blind. What is the point? Before you share SUPER CHANGE principles, ensure your audience self-defines. Are you more comfortable resisting SUPER CHANGE or embracing SUPER CHANGE? You will know them by their works.

Your individual stress loads will fall away as you embrace these SUPER CHANGE mindsets and begin the journey into your superior futures. Such leaders will become the foundation of a thrilling, ever-renewing lifestyle, now and forever moving forward. You will spend your life with awake Super Brain leaders, and your community will be the most exciting cross-mentor community for your own personal growth, because you set up never-ending brain software upgrade process by *choice*.

...nothing wonderful happens until a leader makes their best choice...

CHAPTER 6

THE NEW AGE IS HERE AND IT IS SUPER CHANGE

THE DEMANDS ON MANAGEMENT—IN CORPORATE, institutional, not-for-profit, and civic spaces—are extreme today. This is especially true if your model fails to embrace the new training requirement to stay current. The new priority in management training for executive skill adaptability is SUPER CHANGE leadership mastery. Integrity management, with open transparency, also is required to advance leading edge SUPER CHANGE leadership.

Leadership, in today's SUPER CHANGE age, must be able to circle their silo wagons—in any space from a Fortune institution to a three-person law office—with highly adaptable teams. These teams need to talk about the core principles expressed by SUPER CHANGE leadership, including:

Integrity-based Management: A model based on self-correction and open transparency up and down the ladder.

Self-correction Systems: A culture based on SUPER CHANGE integrity in C-suite leadership. Hub management versus pyramidal management of the past. Policies of recognition, reward, and celebration replacing fear, punishment, and exploitation cultures. The old model is Ebenezer Scrooge and Bob Cratchit (see the movie *A Christmas Carol*). Scrooge's brain upgraded, but that required ghosts of Christmas Past, Present, and Future. Perhaps you need a ghostly vision to take action for your own future into SUPER CHANGE, and perhaps much richer holidays will follow.

Over-compliance Policies: A system based on over-complying with all jurisdictional, legal, tax, environmental, and/or trading partner laws, to set moral and ethical examples for their communities. Integrity and self-compliance are cooperative prides of inspired SUPER CHANGE leadership.

Social Capital: A *cooperative* system model based on community excellence, an open contribution culture, and strong environmental policies. Increasingly, New Brain circles refuse to support trade or alliances with Old Brain competitive leadership supply lines and institutions. Avoiding institutions that commit crimes against nature are choices you make because you change the world for the better when you act in SUPER CHANGE. The scale of this social change is accelerating. The largest financial institutions are seeing that the old competitive model to commit economic crimes is not working, as consumers—awake to Super Change—fire the criminals from their circles and trade up to institutions who have ethics, integrity, and no crime records. Wells Fargo bank and its many years of crimes, and Deutsche Bank (who cannot get a merger partner without help from New Brains), are rotting from the deposit base in the SUPER CHANGE.

Their experts are Old Brains, and they cannot see the future with new glasses. Warren Buffet invested in the criminal bank, Wells Fargo, and his investment has not performed as envisioned. Why invest large sums in criminal leadership cultures? Old Brains are dying off faster as New Brains take over. Social employment and capital investing is already the current trend inside SUPER CHANGE economics, now leading the dollar and sense flows of world cooperative capitalism. Larger sums are investing in social capital executions and drying up Old Brain access to capital in all world market spaces. This is a SUPER CHANGE in core economic flows.

Inclusion Policies: A policy based on human capital being developed, recognized, and rewarded instead of exploited. In that vein, competitive employees who are open to SUPER CHANGE retraining can stay, while those who are closed-minded to SUPER CHANGE culture upgrading can, and are, moved to their choice of competitive cultures.

Celebrating Diversity: Precluding punishment of diversity defines switched-on, turned-on SUPER CHANGE cultures. All stakeholders have an interest to upgrade. SUPER CHANGE cultures contribute to protecting those switched-on, turned-on cultures in every workspace where such principles are engaged. Are you active or passive in your own pace of SUPER CHANGE?

Cultural Policies: A paradigm based on established, deep-diving, repetitive reinforcement and calls to action that create and maintain SUPER CHANGE cultures in the workspace. All stakeholders associated with SUPER CHANGE cultural foundations form a kind of magic management "wagon wheel" of hub management theory, for all internal and external partnerships. Every team supporting you thinks like owners. Focus obsesses on what more we can do for our customers. Everyone is switched-on and turned-on in a workspace with safety nets to upgrade Old Brains or delete them from the culture when they display competitive dynamics and refuse to upgrade their brain software.

Renewal Policies: A process based on mandated systemic renewal of these policies—internally for management and externally for stakeholders and suppliers. Systemic renewal programs are the missing "leadership elevator" to the penthouse of SUPER CHANGE excellence. The blueprint for these renewal pathologies in home space or workspace is outlined in *Redemption: The Cooperation Revolution* for tomorrow's leaders who want details on how to begin. The book contains step-by-step priority sequences and discusses *how* the steps are proven to work in every application, no exceptions. SUPER CHANGE culture reform in your workspace now is affecting all of us. SUPER CHANGE is vastly accelerating. Can you feel the acceleration and G-forces on your brain?

To begin to take action in your workspace, first measure over eight weeks or fewer how your SUPER CHANGE culture installation is proceeding. Define how cooperative your system model is today. Next, as you assess and measure, make notes on how you would modify system review and employee interaction to secure higher performance and absolute adaptation to new SUPER CHANGE cultures. Define how you will make SUPER CHANGE exciting as a personal growth and brand experience evolution system wide. Then, adopt and post this phrase: "Adopt SUPER CHANGE and we all thrive together." This will become your first motto in a SUPER CHANGE culture that will embrace this one phrase... because everyone gets it. We travel on spaceship Earth. Ten billion of us coming up next. We cannot get off spaceship Earth. Spaceship Earth is flying through an extinction rock storm right now. SUPER CHANGE is the new age of our existence on Earth. SUPER CHANGE may save us.

Rule #1: Embrace SUPER CHANGE and we will thrive together.

Rule #2: Never act to depreciate the celebration of our brand in the marketplace.

Rule #3: Celebrate diversity in any form, faith, creed, education, income, size, stature, sex, stuff, and status, anything that diversifies a human. Celebrate and *never punish* human diversity.

In the rip tide of SUPER CHANGE, one sees "whistleblowers" accepting paychecks in a trust, and then trashing their brand in personal competition with leadership. These groups harm the brand. It is not activism. It is not a workplace *right*. It is failure in cooperative culture dynamics and a breakdown of collective trust. It is a breach of integrity agreements to get a paycheck.

Such brand bashers should be finally paid the day of brand harm. No one pays talent to damage the brand that pays them. How insane is that as a culture? Such a breach of trust is a form of insanity and values personal power over collective good.

There are private expressions that can reveal weaknesses in any organization that allow the strength of the institution to repair itself and come to full power. If you accept pay from a brand, you are trusted to take no action that would harm that brand. If you act out to harm the brand with less than the full information, you breach trust and are undeserving of community inclusion. You fail to resolve problems in ways that magnify the brand.

Integrity in the workspace is the crisis today. Why? Competitive expressions that are insane economics created by insane brains and have toxic outcomes. Ask the folks at Google, Facebook, or Microsoft—who founded the firm, took all the risks, created all the futures, wealth, and employment—exactly how betrayed they feel from brand bashing. The people they paid do the bashing? Really? Are you kidding me?

Traitors are always competitive and demonstrate a lack of character and loyalty. Integrity software displays in contrast. If you see fellow workspace actors taking action to harm your brand, bring it to the attention of HR at once. They have policies to upgrade those brains or remove brand traitors who breached their employee agreements. It should be resolved by everyone signing agreements to receive paychecks as consideration. Traitors have no rights in the workspace. Traitors and brand bashers need to stop taking pay and walk the plank to ever-more toxic competitive pastures, where they belong.

SUPER CHANGE resides in higher standards of accountability for human loyalty to the brands that pay them.

Second, install SUPER CHANGE training. You can do this internally with expert SUPER CHANGE certified leadership and culture authorities. Ideally, many will be graduates of CEO Space because we are the industry leader in corporate training for installing SUPER CHANGE cultures in any size workspace. Read the bestselling works, *Transforming Power: Stories from Transformational Leaders for Encouragement and Inspiration* by Fortune corporate culture change expert Hugh Ballou; *The New IQ: How Integrity Intelligence Serves*

You, Your Relationships and Our World by Dr. David Gruder; David Corbin's work, *Illuminate: Harnessing the Positive Power of Negative Thinking;* both *Redemption: The Cooperation Revolution* and *Super Achiever Mindsets,* by Berny Dohrmann; and the must-read *Busting Loose from the Money Game* by Robert Scheinfeld. I favor economics globally with required reading of *The Killing of Uncle Sam* by Rodney Howard-Browne, so you know the landscape into which you are SUPER CHANGING. In this book, the war of Old Brains and New Brains is outlined with research you will find beyond questioning. Each of these texts will help you get ready for this powerful, profitable, performance-enhancing, system-wide culture installation and serve as references after the installation.

You can send executives to training at any of the five annual CEO Space conferences. These are one of the many offers available in this SUPER CHANGE space. From 2010 to 2020, CEO Space's five business growth conferences—which has served 150 nations of CEOs for over thirty years now—has been ranked the number one must-attend business conference by third-party press globally. As I mentioned earlier, other SUPER CHANGE events CEO Space International endorses include those events hosted by Greg Reid and Tony Robbins as leading products, along with Eric Swanson's Habitude Warriors, and Sharon Lechter's Think Big Movement. Find your SUPER CHANGE watering hole and drink drink up. Upgrade your mental software. We all require our own process. We have named many others along your read as reminders. Pick your culture fit.

What is your process to remain current in the unfolding SUPER CHANGE? Do you not have one? *Then choosing yours is your next leadership priority.* Nothing comes before the mindsets that now define winning or losing outcomes from this choice to elevate performance. Prioritize investing in your select process of SUPER CHANGE tools and tactics. Prioritize time to start. Prioritize the frequency of your upgrade in the process. Upgrade in consistent intervals.

However, avoid the "used car sales" folks in this training marketspace, who will upsell something else to you. Their content is not current and their hard-upsell policies may, and most probably do, violate the law. CEO Space, for example, has a "zero upsell" policy. Did you know that training firms who upsell are required by law to provide written disclosure to you about the high commissions paid to the host? This is usually fifty percent of your cost of the item, which is often $10,000 or more. Under the law, the disclosure must include the terms of the fee share (so you know before you go) and precisely what the pay-out is before they offer the product to you. Failure to tell you this in writing *before* every offer gives you the absolute right to a full refund, which includes the government (FTC) assessed fines and penalties. This is defined in the Federal Trade Commission (FTC) rules and is enforced by the new super agency protecting consumers. In fact, if you are a victim of upsell practices like this, and you did not know that fifty percent or more of your upsell purchase was being split with the conference host, contact the FTC—they will get your money back for you. File a complaint. It is your right and it is the law. I see so many burned out, trying to upgrade in SUPER CHANGE, but finding they lost their nest egg, retirement savings, investments, and mortgage their real estate, often investing from one hundred thousand dollars to over one million dollars or more in programs, and having nothing at all to show for those lost dollars today. That upselling was probably illegal. You have a right to your money back. Did you know *that*? Ask an attorney. Show them this paragraph with your highlighter.

If you have invested tens of thousands of dollars or more in hard upsell events or upsell offers, and the firm failed to inform you through a written disclosure that they are paid huge commissions by every seller appearing on their stage, you can sue to get your funds back and still report the party to the FTC. You can file class action lawsuits. See a litigation law firm as it costs nothing to explore your protected legal rights. Spread the word. When attending remote trainings, perform your due diligence to see what third parties ranking the presenters have to say. Check out rip off reports. Due diligence. Check on lawsuits. Do they have unresolved consumer complaints or litigation against them? Do they have top-tier proven mentors who are vetted by third parties? If they upsell, do they present the specifics of the upsell in writing prior to each offer, as required by law? In the end, the buyer must always beware. You must enforce your legal rights. If you do not, you lose.

I've encountered countless instances of third party business owners with over one hundred thousand dollars in credit card and related debt (even second mortgages on their real estate) from having bought into upsells at high-pressure sell events. For most of them who succumbed to hard selling, they made emotional, instead of financial, decisions. Knowing their legal rights and protections would have been enormously helpful to them.

CEO Space carries the highest Better Business Bureau (BBB) ranking. We are a Chamber of Commerce Member in good standing, and we are ranked by *Forbes Magazine*—and a long list of other third-party press, such as *Inc. Magazine*—as the top-ranked business conference in the world from 2010 to 2020. Our conferences are truly press-ranked number one globally, and carry the highest ranking in our industry with zero litigations and no unresolved CEO complaints that we know of. CEO Space is an exclusive club for CEO SUPER CHANGE education. For silo leaders in larger institutions, see our corporate programs, both low cost and lifetime, represent the best corporate value in training executives on the market today.

While other leadership education recommendations named earlier support all levels of C-suite managers, CEO Space limits its lifetime ongoing education service membership to CEO leaders, government division heads, institutional division heads, professionals in practice, small business owner CEOs; and solo entrepreneurs and heads of not-for-profits. Step up to unmatched weeks of mentorship. CEO Space complies with state and federal regulations under a monitored, self-correcting, over-compliance policy. Many leading law firms instruct at CEO Space, and they consistently monitor the compliance levels. Partners of some of the largest law firms, past board member leaders of Booz Allen, and major accounting firms and founding partners of consultants like Accenture, keep CEO Space faculty unique in the mentor space for our members. The firms we have recommended in SUPER CHANGE have all been advised by CEO Space of the FTC rules, though we do not monitor their individual compliance policies which are under their management's direction.

All our faculty are fully vetted by third party due diligence firms, and we endorse them all. The reports appear publicly at www.cleardirectory. com. Tony Robbins, a CEO Space member, is not vetted, but come on, he is *Tony*, and he attended to get new IP, not to teach on faculty. Tony's works and books lead SUPER CHANGE and we work in collaboration on IP to help our respective products. Keep in mind, if Tony upsells his other products, there is no split with third parties. The products are discounted in order to serve his customer base with maximum value. That is why Tony carries our highest SUPER CHANGE endorsement for content to upgrade your home space and workspace. Trust Tony Robbins to SUPER CHANGE every product every single time to *more*.

Retooling your culture with a systemic management model is exciting. It is a fresh renewal for any organization's performance, for any size or age venture. In the era of SUPER CHANGE, delay is a cost too expensive to pay.

Is your online strategy, if you are a small business, presently creating fifty percent or more of your annual revenue? CEO Space recommends Blink of Orlando, Florida, with Daniel Ruke's Fortune expertise breeding *supersites*; sites that attract your customers in SUPER CHANGE with tool kits to convert clicks to sales. Also, from New Zealand, whirlpool sites and social strategies with the Lady Ball Program, hosted by SUPER CHANGE CEO Space leader, Jody Jalis, are two superior options for your online prosperity. Lower budget firms can explore Tafgraphics in Atlanta; you will be SUPER CHANGE accommodated.

Today's Growth Consultant (TGC) upgrades standard websites to supersite status with high-velocity, social-storm-capturing, maximized, lead-to-sale conversions. The leading firm in the industry for institutional and Fortune clients is Solution Stream of Salt Lake City. Check out their roster of clients, from Fortune companies down to hyper-growth brands you know and respect. CEO Space encourages underperforming web upgrade in early SUPER CHANGE explorations. It costs nothing to just explore. For Fortune firms, we suggest Solution Stream. For anti-hacking, only one firm carries our CEO Space endorsement, as does the leader, Phyllis Newhouse of Xtreme Solutions of Atlanta. No other protection even comes close. Phyllis is a prayer partner every Friday and a mentor for years whom I respect. SUPER CHANGE brains and institutions that fit every wallet to upgrade your online presence to its SUPER CHANGE future. Always changing and improving. Check it out!

Andy Marshall, Senior VP of Solution Stream, can help you explore upgrading your online experience so that markets get in line for your brand. Explore EMS Incorporated. Contact Marsha Friedman regarding worldwide public relations media promotions to drive your brand to your core market so that every dollar works like five dollars. I use Blink for CEO Space, and I have used EMS Incorporated since 1991, including on this book's promotions. Trust our vetted resources who will help you remain in SUPER CHANGE.

You may also explore with Cheryl Snapp Connors print promotions and PR on the West Coast. We use Cheryl and have for years. Over time, you can raise your brand awareness and develop one dollar to work like five dollars and drive your customer base to your now-upgraded supersite that is ever-fresh and improving *by design* in SUPER CHANGE. Even more efficient is to use these firms and consultants to revise your online brand presence to become a revenue powerhouse. It costs nothing to explore and get a missing strategy. You will come away with new ideas for what will work, and understand why what you have now is not working ideally. Why again? Just *taking the step* to explore is a SUPER CHANGE outcome choice and is valuable for my readers. Keep this vetted, outstanding reference list handy. Tell them CEO Space sent you and your VIP pass will be implied in the service they provide to you.

These recommended firms are SUPER CHANGE masters and will bring your brand more current in the online, digital, rapidly changing AI marketspace. Far more importantly, they will keep you current as the market changes over short time spans.

If you fail to make week-to-week upgrades to your website, irrespective of your budget constraints, you will fail to catch and ride the SUPER CHANGE bullet train. It is like you are traveling in a covered wagon while SUPER CHANGE is passing by in a Tesla. You become irrelevant in your brand space.

You are either growing in SUPER CHANGE or rotting in old spaces. Which one are you?

SUPER CHANGE guides you, our reader, to re-assess your position. If you resist SUPER CHANGE, you do so due to old software running on the computer above your neck, installed by humans you no longer know and no longer remember, in most cases. This old, buggy, frequently crashing software is no longer safe for you. Is your life blue screening and are you rebooting it over and over? Failure to adapt to SUPER CHANGE is the leading over-stress upon individuals, marriages, and workspace teams today. This tired, obsolete, antique, and buggy software code is making your personal and workspace life dysfunctional. It is also crashing your dreams. Old software is making a life where your future is blue screen crashing over and over... where your life is forever rebooting. As you go about rebooting your precious lifetime, you lose the essential momentum of your most critical asset, which is the lifetime within which the majority of SUPER CHANGE resisters reside in frustration. You are squandering your literal "life time" until you force an upgrade to your buggy, old, SUPER CHANGE-resisting mental software.

Your wealth is your life *time* and the quality of your lifetime versus all the other stuff. I know very affluent families with more stuff than you can list in one book who are miserable. I know folks all over the world with no stuff who are living a life in peace, joy, and bliss. Life time quality is first choice.

You must also adopt the first quality of SUPER CHANGE, which is *urgency*. You must fight the tendency to avoid change. Replace the concept of changing your mental software with the concept of improving your existing mental software capacity by upgrading the software of your mind. Mental software upgrading is a mark of an inspired leader. Inspired SUPER CHANGE leaders are part of switched-on, turned-on institutions that *serve* better; they are also committed to urgent and frequent software upgrades so that they remain current and relevant. These leaders retain a cutting-edge performance outcome that Old Brains can never match. New Brain thinking is an advanced tool chest of opportunities that are not accessible to Old Brain thinkers. Your leadership is forever improved when your brain embraces SUPER CHANGE.

SUPER CHANGE is the age that defines us for the remainder of our futures together. *Human survival rests on our capacity to adapt to change.* With AI as our latest invention, we now pass our own elastic wetware capacity to simply adapt. Change is too immersive, a swirling tornado of change affecting every aspect of our lives moving forward to 2050 and beyond. Our future, our human survival, depends on seeking support, becoming aware in order to remove SUPER CHANGE resistance, and replace such resistance with better whole-brain software until we embrace SUPER CHANGE.

Leaders in the SUPER CHANGE market space invest time and resources on continuously upgrading their own mental software. Find your tribe. Choose your process. Build a SUPER CHANGE, cooperation-oriented circle of mentors and team players. Avoid those who are not like-minded. Pay far more attention to your team's mindsets. Research and find your own ongoing training tribe of mentors, on-site and off-site, as you will require both. Create and live inside of SUPER CHANGE communities that better serve you and that thrill you.

Then commit to a frequency and urgency to install new, better-performing software, quarterly at least.

Reading this book is a software upgrade by itself. Sharing this work upgrades software for your community and your circle of customers and stakeholders.

Upgrade your software as soon as you can. This is a time when weeks are like years, months are like decades, and years are like centuries when you delay SUPER CHANGE software upgrades. *Use time differently.* As leaders upgrade their core leadership competency density quarter-to-quarter, their teams will exert more market relevance and adaptability. New Brain leader competency density will explode.

Financial institutions are an example of diminishing competency density. They are generating returns for their mass investor clients that are at the lowest level in a century. Inefficient Old Brain systems, which they have failed to upgrade, run their models. Their integrity crisis is made obvious in the movie *The Big Short*. The result is that these institutions, not all, but many, still fail to meet the market investor demands for a value of eight percent returns or higher for capital invested. As the record earnings for banks continues to soar, the depositors make decade-low returns. Why? Outdated software that is not sustainable long-term. Old competitive economics exploit their clients. SUPER CHANGE institutions serve their clients better. If you are a proud and competitive institution, if you kick your dog enough under the table, one day, your dog will move.

Further, they create products that are short-term manipulations. They are toxic for society, anti-social, and driven by antique notions of abusive bonus and compensation plans. They are kicking all of us like dogs. These products place the abusers in direct competition with their own capital source: their client. Old Brain software has put their century-old and older brand in competition with their customers, and the inefficiency of such market positioning only expands over time. The result is that the entire financial system is at risk, as SUPER CHANGE is unforgiving of systemic abuse in social capital or social quality. Old Brain leaders committed crimes against humanity in financial institutions we used to trust. They created phony accounts to make bonus money and deceive shareholders. They fixed interest prices illegally. They designed false emission auto control systems to deceive regulatory officials. They used their unique positions and public trust to earn trillions collectively. Old Brains always display a lack of integrity, a lack of regard for social capital, and a loss of core vision for future customer service and maximum customer value exchange. Major financial institutions are rotting and new institutions with lower cost and integrity on privacy—say, in super-changing generational blockchain evolutions—are removing Old Brains and changing commerce. This commerce was locked into, "That is the way we have always done it." Are you rotting from the inside of your Old Brain to the outside of your Old Brain today? Old Brains have issues with accepting responsibility. They reside in victim space where they consider their crimes misunderstandings, while their greed wastes billions of dollars.

Financial institutions *are* rotting due to a lack of adaptation to SUPER CHANGE, and by basing their organizational theory on competition versus cooperation HUB management. This is known to Amazon but not to Citigroup. I often speak with CEO Space faculty member Ron Klein, who invented the magnetic strip on the credit card. SUPER CHANGE comes to commerce. Then comes the chip. Now biometrics.

You either embrace and thrive inside SUPER CHANGE, or you resist and you will rot. Your state of thinking starts and stops with your mindset. Do you understand your mindset? Finding out the *accurate answer* is your most important next step. You may need some help.

This work presents methods to retool your C-suite thinkers and silo CEOs so they hold a higher regard for the skillful adaptation you lead to their upgraded mental capacity into SUPER CHANGE. For development-stage entrepreneurs, my favorite books for you are:

Pivot: The Art and Science of Reinventing Your Career and Life, by Adam Markel. Also, from Singapore, one of the largest personal development firms in the world, now owned by Richard Tan, founder of Success Resources and his amazing SUPER CHANGE wife Veronica.

More books for your SUPER CHANGE list:

Three Feet From Gold: Turn Your Obstacles into Opportunities! (*Think and Grow Rich* series), by Sharon Lechter and co-authored by Greg Reid.

The *Rich Dad Poor Dad* series, *Think and Grow Rich for Women*, and *Outwitting the Devil*, all by Sharon Lechter.

Performance Driven Selling, and other books by Jeff Magee.

Busting Loose by Robert Scheinfeld, with a foreword from Jack Canfield, and Jack's *Success Principles*. Finally, all of Tony Robbins's works and Bob Proctor's works. SUPER CHANGE leaders all.

These SUPER CHANGE authors also serve as CEO Space legacy faculty, mentors and members, save for *Busting Loose*, and we believe he will join CEO Space faculty when we ask him.

The squandering of life opportunities at home and in workspaces is staggering. This is the source of all current stress and wheel wobble issues. The actual cause of your problems is masked by many symptoms, and results in a failure to adapt to SUPER CHANGE. Look backwards; it helps you see forward with perspective from your rearview mirror of self-assessment. In the SUPER CHANGE age, the demands of leadership represent an entirely new rulebook from the obsolete "once upon a time" university models of yesterday. As every SUPER CHANGE leader knows, the penalty of leadership is universal and seriously challenging, and in the 2020 decade, it is no fairy tale, and it is not for the faint-hearted leader.

Redemption: The Cooperation Revolution defines how C-suite executives can reform culture from competitive, lower-performing output to higher performing cooperative organizations and truly switched-on, turned-on workspace institutions. The output gains from these culture upgrades are more dramatic than from any other priority consideration CEOs can direct. No other priority comes first. No other priority affects output and performance faster.

Culture reform elevates performance throughout the workspace as well as the home space.

Change your mind and you will find the new gold mine is in the *mind* field, not the minefield. Be a great miner as you discover how to fully mine your own mind.

Education is a lifelong requirement of those who lead... we grow or we go....

CHAPTER 7

SUPER CHANGE LEADERS REPRESENT THE GOLD MINDS OF TOMORROW

INCREASINGLY, BOARDS OF DIRECTORS DEFINE their fiduciary first responsibility as developing the new policy and management templates of SUPER CHANGE measurement and assessment. Desired performance gains have become impossible outside a SUPER CHANGE workspace culture and leadership board policy.

Those who lack a top-tier SUPER CHANGE process (given top-tier products from Tony Robbins to Steve Farber of LQ, to Chris Wise in San Francisco via Jack Maas's SUPER CHANGE engineering) are left behind on the unfolding SUPER CHANGE score cards of their stakeholders. Shareholders are demanding SUPER CHANGE board leadership, and SUPER CHANGE managers/owners, and the source of future common vision in shorter time cycles, to renew and source future corporate outcomes. Investors are avoiding those enterprises that do not know what SUPER CHANGE is, and whose antique, university-damaged CEOs are left behind in all markets.

This antiquated state of being applies to nations as well as institutions in the SUPER CHANGE era. Soaring risk is moderated by being forever SUPER CHANGE current, SUPER CHANGE bleeding edge, and SUPER CHANGE up-to-date, or by leaders who are terrified of being out of date. Leaders *know* if they are being left in the dust. The reason: failure to engage a top-tier process to become current, because such process offers also maintain leaders and keep them current in the changing global marketspaces. This age you are in is here now, it is accelerating while you read, and your tactic and process to lead appropriately with SUPER CHANGE skill sets is a weeks-away, not months-away, decision.

Have you clicked, explored, and decided on your own best fit and process customized for your tribe with stats and expertise at your level? This includes entrepreneurial leaders planning development and pre-launch, to mature Fortune 100 leaders at the top of the pile. No one remains current without consistent mental software upgrading into SUPER CHANGE processes that account for the unique and new stress points on leadership. If you are applying Ford Model T leadership into a forward SUPER CHANGE global marketplace, you will lose opportunity. If you upgrade continuously, you will grow more rapidly than if you do not engage your process. Awake and knowledgeable SUPER CHANGE boards demand higher-tier SUPER CHANGE management.

Today the boss is the gold *mind*, not a gold *mine in the ground*. With the right mindset, we can make gold and diamonds ourselves, helping Mother Nature out in her knowledge.

The software the boss is using to make decisions, as never before, is a business endowment that requires a continuous process of upgrading. Ideally, a quarter-to-quarter gym for the boss's mental software is suggested. Programs like CEO Space, Tony Robbins' events, *Secret Knock*, Sharon Lechter's Think Big Movement, Eric Swanton's Habitude Warrior, as well as growing retreats from new leaders coming in today, and others, provide lessons on establishing and sustaining the ability and agility to be and to remain current.

The full list of CEO Space alliance partnerships, available at www.
ceospaceinternational.com, presents fully vetted and wonderful options
to upgrade leadership software, suitable for any stage of leadership.
CEOs of larger institutions tell the CEO Space faculty that their double
Wharton credentials and their refreshers at forty thousand dollars
a pop were exceeded in their first CEO Space upgrade experience.
Testimonials at all levels, from Fortune C-suites to development space
ventures that are the unicorns of tomorrow, flow through CEO Space.
Your task is to find your:

- Content
- Context
- Click Factor
- Culture Match

Super Change presents options for experts, options for process
offers, and endorsements for customized matches to who you *are*
today as a leader. Leaders are alone and under-appreciated. It is the
new normal for leaders be over-stressed. Leaders often have lives that
do not thrill them. Leaders are challenged to keep pace and to renew
brand authority more quickly than ever before in the shifting sands in
all brand space in SUPER CHANGE.

Use any combination of these resources to secure your own
SUPER CHANGE state-of-the-art software process.

Adapting to SUPER CHANGE requires ongoing upgrading for silo
leaders in your team circles. I ask *you* as the leader you are today,
again:

What is your process to ensure leaders remain current in the new
age of SUPER CHANGE? If you lack a process suitable to your culture,
do your research and adopt that one that feels like the best match for
who you are today. Network with Super Brain leaders you admire and
ask their recommendation on external and internal processes.

All the process suggestions we provide in SUPER CHANGE are vetted and they work. Each process offered leads to other options, too. Share this work with other leaders and grow your community of leaders who are on the same page in SUPER CHANGE. The number of SUPER CHANGE leaders is now becoming the majority, and Old Brains are becoming the minority. This is one of the most significant leadership improvements in human history, taking place since 2010, with massive traction since 2015. The leadership conversation has shifted.

Today, you must know *how* to make improvements in your mental software, and you must secure that new information even while a stream of new opportunities for your business are compressed in ever-accelerating SUPER CHANGE terms. Making invisible options become visible to leadership is a benefit of your selected SUPER CHANGE process. In SUPER CHANGE, yesterday is already too late to begin...

Delay is the cost old leadership pays. This is a price SUPER CHANGE leaders never pay because they know the price is a staggering sum of lost options for stakeholders. Old Brain leadership in institutions such as, Pan American Airlines or Eastern Airlines or Montgomery Ward, all once dominant brands, have gone up in SUPER CHANGE smoke today; and also, as we said, Toys "R" Us, Circuit City, and Sears; for how the mighty who miss it fall. The cause is weak plans, weak teams, and missing resources within a mental leadership software that has become irrelevant due to lack of a process to remain current as a leader in the new age of SUPER CHANGE. Today, currency in the C-suite is the bar of gold in leadership of tomorrow.

See stores and chains and global brands all evaporate into failure by not upgrading into the new age of SUPER CHANGE. None of us can get out of moving forward. Institutions I grew up with are all gone today because of their failure to adapt. For example, the once-dominant brands such as Kodak or General Motors. Their investors, stakeholders, loyal customers, employees, and more all went up in smoke for failing to adapt to SUPER CHANGE.

The penalty for failure to adapt is becoming an economic ratio of compressing timeframes.

Will Microsoft, Facebook, and Apple become victims or winners in the accelerating SUPER CHANGE they helped create? The failure to lead and bleed in SUPER CHANGE begins in the boardroom and in the mind fields of the SUPER CHANGE leaders they elect. The crisis in all nations remains education failing to present tools and tactics to prosper inside the new age of SUPER CHANGE. They have zero curriculum on the topic. CEO Space will license the Entrepreneur Curriculum 2000 module to help education globally.

You are reading the last chapter of the first book ever written on the topic we have labored on with global Fortune leadership for four decades. We defined the age, we led the tools and tactics that reach millions today. We started a cooperation revolution in the 1980s, which has advanced to the majority of organizations today, because cooperative systems modeling and cultures outperform failed competitive system models and cultures. We are happier in switched-on, turned-on SUPER CHANGE-led workspaces. I know I am.

The majority of small business owners are missing the tools and tactics that larger institutions in this SUPER CHANGE space can apply and afford. Re-training corporate cultures an industry has risen from eighty billion dollars in revenues to a projected one trillion dollar industry worldwide by 2030. The SUPER CHANGE training industry is a top-ten GNP product in over one hundred nations today. This industry did not exist when we started it all in the 1980s.

However, a growing number of small businesses are, in 2020, using one or more of the SUPER CHANGE upgrading programs that deliver ability and mental agility in establishing and sustaining being current at the top of the C-suite leadership circle. Many of the leading process resources are named here for you to explore at your leisure. Google can provide others until your customized process resource matrix is ever advancing. All of these resources deliver the cornerstone SUPER CHANGE mental agility tools and tactics as the priority C-suite asset. Leaders install SUPER CHANGE currency, within SUPER CHANGE cultures, to maintain their workspaces. This work to your employees, suppliers, and stakeholders begins the unifying discussion.

Who is teachable, with a leadership teachable spirit? Who is not?

Bosses secure alliances, affiliates, and marketing joint ventures when they allocate adequate time to grow their SUPER CHANGE community and SUPER CHANGE workspace capital. This culture investment drives performance gains and profits. A boss reinvents the vision of the entity to the ever-accelerating new SUPER CHANGE marketspace, thereby elevating customer outcomes. The boss creates new expanded profit offers for its existing customer base and improves customer experiences.

Communities of business owners are now the future of remaining current—they are working on your venture box growth versus being fully trapped inside your venture box. Leading brains quickly spot improved or missing options and new opportunities while they make invisible options visible to the communities they serve. For years, CEO space has endorsed social capital institutions like *Vistage*, the Women Presidents' Organization, *Woman of Wealth* magazine, and George Frasier's annual conferences, Power Teams, to grow CEO-to-CEO social capital. Social capital and vision planning are the core tasks of a CEO. Execution of the vision plan on timelines is a task of the CEO team.

Social capital promotes sharing best practices to get the jobs done on timelines that work. By using both *collaboration and cooperation* as culture in social capital, SUPER CHANGE CEOs grow so much faster than those who fail to invest the time to renew mental agility and grow skills that allow them to stay current in SUPER CHANGE mental capital.

SUPER CHANGE leaders all know how hard it is to lead under the unrelenting pressures of SUPER CHANGE. CEOs helping one another, in social community, substantially lighten the load for each other and expedite growth through resource sharing and improving the mental agility required of advanced SUPER CHANGE leaders who are committed to their own process of currency.

CEOs today must create ventures, including government silos, which obsess on their client benefits to the exclusion of all other priorities. Today, AI in SUPER CHANGE punishes leaders who fail to reach their set timelines for outcomes. Leaders who fail to upgrade customer outcomes are punished by the marketplace that is experience loyal and no longer brand loyal. What worked in one age does not work in another age.

AI rewards leaders who get it right in real time within the new AI SUPER CHANGE marketplace, and AI will now create maximum instant punishment or reward new markets in SUPER CHANGE based on its own red lines.

Super volatility in economic markets is a new-normal inside SUPER CHANGE markets. Read about the current SUPER CHANGE interpretation of fake news worldwide, all spun to manipulate voter outcomes. www.bernydohrmann.com is a free public service for my readers. Free to subscribe or make a bookmark. Knowledge in SUPER CHANGE is power if you have that knowledge first. Share this SUPER CHANGE blog that presents news in context of the global entwinement of economics. SUPER CHANGE leaders have greater mental agility, make better quality decisions, and use blogs to apply better information to lower risk outcomes in SUPER CHANGE markets affecting their home office or global operations. Make a bookmark and subscribe. I reply to all comments personally.

AI today controls ninety-six percent of $440 trillion in global placements and flows. From 2014 to 2020, the economics moved from systems developed over one hundred years with humans in full control, to systems invented in only five years, bypassing central banks and nations. AI is now in total control with no human involved whatsoever. This experiment in core economics has now spawned a new economic system, the AI economics of the future, for which no nation has oversight regulations or even, in most cases, is yet aware SUPER CHANGE has absolutely changed core global economics.

SUPER CHANGE is stressing institutions and nations and is changing core economics on scales and timeframes human beings have never known before. Universities remain trapped in the quicksand of, paper-managed economic theory, which is completely dead, retired, and well buried. The Milton Friedman and Keynesian economics I studied are all mummies today, gone with the economies of Egypt and of Rome. Those economics have been proven to be wrong. Old economics is toxic to new economics. Central banks are in yellow *use caution* without new SUPER CHANGE leadership brains on their governing boards of directors. Think about Old Brain economists making central bank policy in the AI SUPER CHANGE new economic theory. Nothing works as expected.

Yet this obsolete and failed economic theory is still considered gospel today at universities. That education is now toxic, it is like teaching graduates how to use a rock and slingshot in a world of SAWS and fifty-caliber automatics that vests will not stop. How does the FED leader with a slingshot not get torn to shreds by AI automatic weapons. We saw this as the decade turned, did we not? Central banks lacking SUPER CHANGE upgraded mentally agile leadership are presenting Ford Model T tools—"That's the way we always did it."—into a Starship, anti-matter, new AI economy for which the world has no context. The AI is getting smarter and smarter, as are the economic state warfare tools to digitally attack all markets and profit from those attacks.

Teaching obsolete content to leaders creates leaders who are unprepared to step into their roles without massive re-education to undo the damage of many of today's post-graduate degrees. The SUPER CHANGE universities, which are not available today but are coming online rapidly, will see their product shifting into currency based upon the SUPER CHANGE leaders hired in the future. In the 2020s, the leaders of many Ivy League universities are being fired for buggy mental software and lacking the mental agility required in SUPER CHANGE markets.

SUPER CHANGE is affecting tuition revenue at Keiser University in Florida State because it is a self-correcting, ever upgrading, SUPER CHANGE, family-run institution. The award-winning systemic educational game changer engages models and expertise that embrace SUPER CHANGE. I applaud President Gary Vont, and even more, a standing ovation for Chairman and CEO Art Keiser, and his wife, Belinda, for showing the way forward into what is possible in a top-tier, state-accredited, university with campuses worldwide. They are stepping education systemically into the future in Miami, Florida. SUPER CHANGE class size, faculty recognition reward systems, switched-on, turned-on faculty culture and core SUPER CHANGE curriculums set the tone. Art, your parents and grandparents cannot be more proud of you on your watch today.

Harvard, Yale and Stanford should visit Keiser, along with Georgetown, Pepperdine, and Cornell, for their own modeling upgrades into systemic SUPER CHANGE institutions of the future. Universities such as Keiser are on the way *in*, and Art now has his institution worldwide in the 2020s growing rapidly via affiliates and mergers—from China to the EU. One of the first holistic, education-wide, systemic SUPER CHANGE educational models is an Art and Belinda Keiser invention in culture and modeling. Step into the future of education with a field trip to Keiser, and tell them the author of *Super Change* sent you. Together we will improve the entire world.

Competitive cultures will always underperform against cooperative cultures. Cooperative cultures always outperform competitive cultures.

Board fiduciaries are at risk for failing to upgrade into SUPER CHANGE policy culture and leadership to protect their stakeholder value tables now and in the future.

Assessment applications and reviews now include a leader's SUPER CHANGE index score card. Outcome is measured by SUPER CHANGE indexing to outcomes. Does your process include SUPER CHANGE indexing at every level of participation inside a switched-on, turned-on workspace?

The old assessment model, in competition, measures your steps to the bathroom, break room and vending machines. You are "corrected" for output that is not meeting objective without subjective standard as weight. Each review focuses on criticism to result in behavior modifications to secure longer hours, more work per hour, and more output per day.

The new SUPER CHANGE assessment places context to work and its relationship to the common vision and social contribution. The assessment is weighted on what the stakeholder did right. Within the praise and acknowledgement, small requests are delivered as suggestions that may better elevate the award-winning work the individual is now doing, and you welcome *their* input to secure even more by working smarter not harder. They partner to the whole because they clearly see that they are a part of the whole. They also see over-stress as impersonal and SUPER CHANGE. Because (says the supervisor in SUPER CHANGE reviews) SUPER CHANGE impacted our brand this way and that way since the last reviews, we are securing what makes us lead. Your help to take good to great, which you already did, and great to magnificent, and magnificent to magic, and magic to miracles as the union of purpose and context drives reward and recognition systemic modeling. This upgrade in tone and in process moves toxic competitive talent turnover to holistic talent buy-in. The process never ends.

Coming together for cohesive outcomes is a product of SUPER CHANGE. Cooperative organizational culture models are vastly improved human organizational models, where brands renew and remain relevant inside SUPER CHANGE and profits are growing as more clients are served with pride.

Transforming your culture—in both home spaces and workspaces—into a cooperative space, builds your social capital and continuously accelerates your desired outcomes. Cooperative workspaces will magnify your brand to the all-futures marketplaces. It compresses timelines profitably to keep pace with SUPER CHANGE. This process keeps C-suite leadership fully current, with the new quarterly options and opportunities SUPER CHANGE delivers endlessly. It fosters switched-on, turned-on home spaces and switched-on, turned-on workspaces, that impact performance as the marketplace celebrates your upgrades. It is impossible to foster and maintain a switched-on, turned-on workspace within a competitive pyramid management structure. The cooperation system model always massively outperforms the competitive model. The brain drains and turnover of raw talent, trained at cost, are now exiting in short periods due to system mismatching.

We invite our readers to assess their leadership direction. How current are you, really? What process do you use to grow your core leadership software, while you associate in the superior social capital of high-functioning CEO communities? Communities of SUPER CHANGE leaders cross mentor options and opportunities. Do you have a larger cooperative CEO community you utilize like Vistage (a CEO Space recommendation for qualifying leadership), or do you have other processes?

We suggest that the switched-on leader consider mapping out a new, quarterly process, inside a rapidly accelerating SUPER CHANGE global marketspace. CEOs need to pull their slingshot back tightly, every quarter, to renew the energy required to hit their income target bullseye in ever-compressing timeframes. If your Old Brain slingshot is hanging down and limp, you cannot hit your targets at all, or even the hay bale holding your target income. Timeframes are forever compressing, resulting in leader over-stress as a toxic unwanted outcome for failure to upgrade mental agility in SUPER CHANGE. New tools and new leadership tactics are required, and every brain can easily download them. The only question is when, and what priority do you place first? Better brain software, better decision outcomes. Do you not now see more clearly, upgrading your brain mental agility is first and next, and using your new upgraded brain software to make decisions improves and elevates choice velocity and choice quality for each decision. That priority is next for inspired leaders.

Ask not for whom this bell tolls, for in SUPER CHANGE the bell tolls for out-of-date and obsolete boards and leaders... it tolls for you!

You already know you are proceeding into the future market of challenges never before present in any prior market space. You see it every day. Dealing with SUPER CHANGE is a new, critical path, C-suite-required mindset—the mindset of *transformational* leadership. CEO Space trains other trainers currently leading in the space of transformational leadership. We know you have been exposed to our work without knowing the source. Now you do, as the majority of trainings today, and leading seven-figure Fortune CEO mentors, are graduates of CEO Space. I mention CEO Space because we invented it to bring management current in SUPER CHANGE and keep leaders current. In 1988, at the start of the new age of SUPER CHANGE, we were bleeding edge—leading the first of our kind. From Tony Robbins to Bob Proctor, mentors to CEOs in the Fortune 100 industry, or Old Brain leaders such as Tom Peters who was trained outside CEO Space, CEO Space then retrained Steve Farber out of Tom Peters's tool boxes, and Steve has now trained countless other trainers and brands, to extend those CEO Space tools to our hundreds of thousands of members across 150 nations, leading untold millions into better futures.

Their product offerings, along with those of Greg Reid and Sharon Lechter, are vibrant, new technologies to upgrade leadership. Our work began in the 1990s with AT&T, and down to 3M on the Fortune Chart. One hundred and fifty nations later, CEO Space has outpaced all others. Why? Our ability to upgrade leadership into its most advanced form of problem solving is forged on new tactics and tools for SUPER CHANGE. It adapts every sixty days and upgrades itself. That's right. Listen, we created the first SUPER CHANGE process to upgrade to new SUPER CHANGE in the market. All of us must possess greater mental agility to lead.

We not only invented the solution to the core problem, we stressed upgrading our own CEO Space content for our leaders even then, every sixty days, five times a year. This was the first process of a fully current leadership commitment that was ongoing and never-ending. Pay once, benefit for *life*.

No one else at that time imagined a self-advancing, always-upgrading, continuous training modality. Now, we are finally being copied. The need for our standard of leadership upgrading is far greater than CEO Space can accommodate. CEO Space cannot accommodate even a tiny market share of the rising one trillion dollar annual future training industry itself SUPER CHANGING and soaring in demand.

Our game plan is to secure a family corporate hedge fund pre-IPO partner to invest and partnership-own CEO Space for a one hundred million dollar advertising and marketing capital equity investment. As the earnings and margins soar from positioning the number one press-ranked brand to thirty-nine million entrepreneurs in the USA alone, and 1.7 billion worldwide, CEO Space hyper-grows. Our models include working with major New York firms to grow demand to our factory of SUPER CHANGE CEO accommodations, and benefits to six Dallas convention center ballrooms, and color-coded classes of five thousand CEOs in each class. These wagon wheel classes, where mentor teams rotate between classrooms, secure a thirty thousand five-time-a-year B2B super-tradeshow where business gets done. New markets and capital are secured. The next IPO is to have our own customer base as stockholders, where proceeds of the public firm advanced the proven model to the same five weeks of hosting for the Africa Space, the EU Space, the Asia Space, and the South American Space, complementing the founder forum and the North American space – training up to one million CEO entrepreneurs who, with lifetime memberships, can rotate to CEO Space community on continents they wish to grow within.

The projections of the mature model (which may occur after I am gone, given my age) exceed a billion dollars in annual revenue from streaming content subscriptions and CEO Space memberships. The multiple, if realized as projected, will sustain, in my opinion, ever-rising stock value resulting in education reform in the age of the entrepreneur. This game plan works to keep CEO Space the industry leader to our readers' benefit. Your click to explore includes, while volume allows it, free setup coaching into CEO Space on a Power Hour intensive mentor collaboration with me personally, as my thank you.

To remain number one, we must always upgrade CEO Space, and we do. We lead by example, and I bring it up not to sell it to you but to tell you to follow this bouncing ball. See our endorsed list of process providers, which will lead to more. Pick any of them as CEO Space-endorsed. If you are in doubt, ask us: ellen@ceospaceinternational. com. Over ninety percent of our endorsements are fully vetted by third parties and appear on www.cleardirectory.com. For a small charge, you can access a large faculty with expertise on their resume and a full report on their backgrounds—including my wife, September, and me. This provides you with full transparency to know before you go into anything.

You must bleed and lead by constantly upgrading your own mental agility in SUPER CHANGE. To retrain your brain to learn faster, unlearn even faster, and relearn faster than that takes practice. The more you practice, the more you lead in SUPER CHANGE. Choose your culture fit and process. Click to check out and explore solutions to this next priority—your self-development. SUPER CHANGE training is not an event; it is a process that, once started, must never end. Think about your SUPER CHANGE deficit. Do you have a SUPER CHANGE deficit index for your institution? Do you need help creating one? A SUPER CHANGE deficit index, once an invisible option, has now become visible to you from reading a book. How many have become visible if you highlighted and made margin notes? How priceless are the one or two that were just for you?

For internal training, we invented Super Teaching, a digital classroom to elevate learner retention of core content in industry, education, nation, or military. Click www.superteaching.org to explore Super Teaching for your school systems or institution training centers. Super Teaching technology patents were issued in China and worldwide for a SUPER CHANGE modality for all classroom design seeking higher learner performance. Every training classroom requires Super Teaching technology to elevate learner retention. Super Teaching, we believe, is the New Brain learner classroom favorite of tomorrow by design, accommodating the new digital learner space. Upgrading classrooms to Super Teaching empowers educators like no other tool in the world, and it was created for the classroom of tomorrow. We license source code at low cost to any education request—you agree in open source to provide fully annotated and upgraded source code to our teams—to place the genius of the world of education, to make Super Teaching software clients SUPER CHANGE, with educators leading what they alone *know* they need and desire next. This is a low-cost revolution in upgrading SUPER CHANGE and super teaching classrooms of tomorrow. In 2010, CEO Space donated a classroom to the University of Alabama, yet another higher learning institution. This is one of my own great passions, and Tony Robbins cut the ribbons. Roll Tide.

Once you adapt your teams in a process into SUPER CHANGE, you will discover the process is the most compelling financial up-ramp imaginable for your business. Social capital associations become the boss's most replenishing mental capital possible in the non-static, always-accelerating new age of SUPER CHANGE. Social capital presents ideas to the boss that are impossible outside new community circles that are devoted to successfully processing and dealing with SUPER CHANGE. Social capital as a *product* of embracing SUPER CHANGE exists in new AI economics that benefit customers while making a profit. Short-term profit-making is no longer the goal as that is insane economic modeling. See Uber, Twitter, Pinterest, and other unicorn, public, social, good institutions, with revenues rising and profit every three weeks meaning zero to those leaders. New economics versus old economics. Which are you?

Over the course of thirty years of leading the Forbes-ranked and *Inc. Magazine* number one global business conference, at CEO Space we continually upgrade our own process, and that process is every sixty days dedicated as our core process to teaching leaders like you how to thrive in SUPER CHANGE. Remember the super crash economic bubble of 2007, which is only a short time ago in economic years. As future bubbles are always upon us, leaders find there is safety in numbers, and there is even more safety in like-minded numbers when each financial storm hits them. This provides safe harbors the others lack. Read www.bernydohrmann.com to remain more current with bubbles unfolding globally. Plan accordingly for your safe harbor. We tell leaders how, step-by-step, for free, online. (I love challenge and will reply to you personally.)

Growing non-static, ever-expanding CEO-to-CEO relationships inside organized business acceleration products and events is the future of CEO modernity planning. Keeping the process of upgrading mental leadership development as a priority will grow a priceless CEO community. CEO community in SUPER CHANGE is the single greatest risk reducer and profit enhancer. Do not stay behind the circle you know today. Uncork a CEO community of like-minded individuals who are in SUPER CHANGE development with you. Who they are and whom they know will grow your peer-to-peer community and foster the priceless asset of CEO-to-CEO relationships. This is another SUPER CHANGE modality, an essential tool.

No one can stay current from a single event—becoming and staying current is a *process*. C-suite planners need to discover, retain, and participate in their own process to remain current in SUPER CHANGE. We encourage using regular off-site, remote trainings specifically engineered to help C-suite management remain current. The CEO Space model adapts programs to keep up with accelerated CEO pacing. The C-suite team can run their tasks in offices (there are hourly breaks for this purpose) from within the SUPER CHANGE process training, which permits time blocks for existing work obligation. This new model of residency remote training elevates team harmony, deep bonding, problem solving, and accelerated result attainment. What process are *you* planning to use? Use these yardsticks as you compare, as so many advanced and great new programs are coming to market in SUPER CHANGE. Pick your best fit.

Develop your upgrade process and commit to it to become more current and remain bleeding edge. The tools and tactics in SUPER CHANGE are ever-evolving journeys whose destinations are all short term, that unfold in the SUPER CHANGE market space quarter-to-quarter. Planning that fails to deliver goals on time should consider SUPER CHANGE as a weak risk on outcome for attaining the desired goal inside required timelines, on average. Stronger plans, based on SUPER CHANGE, need to be developed and acted upon to reduce unwanted risk of failed performance. With mentor support, SUPER CHANGE leaders are improving plans, elevating execution teams to outcomes, and infusing missing required resources into the on-time goal attainments. Better plans, improved execution team talent, and resource acquisitions is the exclusive CEO fiduciary responsibility to direct, from a naturopathic practice to Morgan Stanley C-suite vision planning to reset its core brand into tomorrow's customer mindsets.

As you think about the principles of SUPER CHANGE, you will define your own path. It is all about new tools and tactics for being the boss. The process is fun and replenishes the depletion so many owners and CEOs feel day-to-day inside the over-stress of resistance to SUPER CHANGE. Social capital for resolving business challenges can come from CEO Space, *Vistage*, the Women Presidents' Organization, George Frasier's Power Networking events, and *Woman of Wealth Magazine* events, among many others named here for your exploration. Tony Robbins's suites of products that my wife and I attend are upgrading leaders of Fortune institutions and individuals in home space relationships. CEO Space endorses and recommends Tony Robbins's corporate and individual process programs for your consideration. Tony works hard on mindset tools. CEO Space works on systemic workspace organization, and tools and tactics to download to remain fully current. What is your resonance to process? There is a toolbox today for every leader's frequency.

We also rest on the wisdom of one of the great performance trainers of our century, multiple *New York Times* bestselling breakthrough author, Dr. Lee Pulos. Dr. Pulos was also a co-inventor with our teams of CEO Space. Dr. Pulos suggests that the world has reached the end of "left-brain problem solving." The problems facing all of us are sufficiently interconnected and complex so that only "right-brain solutions" will resolve these higher-level mental challenges. To this important resolution, the rise of women leaders is essential. It is also obviously important to develop male leaders who embrace their SUPER CHANGE right-brain capacity.

These superior problem-solvers of both genders will elevate women, within cooperative social capital, into full partnership in solving the problem matrix. Elevating "Lady Leaders" at all levels of decision-making when the team functions in a cooperative corporate culture model accelerates quality and quantity for all choices. Social capital—at governance in state, national, and corporate levels—must include women leaders as *full* partners in order to advance the solutions to SUPER CHANGE challenges. Failure to make these social capital adjustments will resist SUPER CHANGE. The consequences may be world war—an obsolete, male-dominated, problem-solving idea that is fully antiquated in the age of SUPER CHANGE.

I know in our CEO Space movement to all-lady leader management, in 2014 we rose from the top business conference list ranking of number 5 (myself and the old-boy board) to the number one slot, year after year, with all-lady managers rocking it! We lead by telling you what works because we are serving 150 nations today that did it first. I encourage you, as a mentor to Fortune CEOs and all sizes of enterprises, sprinkle lady leaders as full partners on your board and C-suite leadership and the future begins to SUPER CHANGE effortlessly for you. Review equal pay for all, and celebrate diversity in your core economic policy plan—a SUPER CHANGE diversity institution.

In fact, war is nothing other than an insane mental software, an expression of extreme insanity for competitive insane thought impulse. Leaders are advised to write a declaration of war email late into the night, read it aloud to a woman, then delete it. Then you will be better in the sanity of morning thought without the competitive impulse on your CPU at all.

Women's leadership will help any organization mark itself as a strong SUPER CHANGE institution. Women leaders will help individuals and institutions choose cooperative sanity over competitive insanity. The lack of women in C-suites and boards of directors is the mark of an antique brain that is taking your brand and investing down the risk hole. Is that you today?

We cannot do the things we have always done and expect to get the results we now truly want. "That is the way we have always done it," inside SUPER CHANGE is the mind mark of real insanity. Is that you? We must do things differently to get the results we desire and require. If we do the things we used to do, and expect new results, we are insane. The sane know they must think differently in SUPER CHANGE. It is not simply an *option* to embrace SUPER CHANGE—it is *sane* to embrace SUPER CHANGE.

As you complete this first-ever book on SUPER CHANGE, ask what you would wish to be different about your venture or your life in order to reach your goals faster? Next, think about speeding up that vision with social capital and acquire your most perfect, resonant, regular SUPER CHANGE process that is in harmony with your culture and personality as a leader. Your choice will always win in SUPER CHANGE. Reform your culture from *competition* to *cooperation* using my book, *Redemption: The Cooperation Revolution,* as the step-by-step workbook for reforming your work and home cultures. Have your teams read *Super Change* to align team support and priorities? Has your social capital circle of suppliers and stakeholders read *Super Change* so everyone is talking from the same playbook? As they gift their best clients with *Super Change*, the culture of embracing SUPER CHANGE goes viral. You are now leading and part of the global SUPER CHANGE movement. Just give ten books as gifts to thank your ten top sources of income. Viral SUPER CHANGE to reward loyalty and cement-in working together to remain current in that foundation of agile mental capital. You will have better decisions all of the time after the first upgrade.

Give yourself a CEO retreat once each quarter to refresh the next quarter's results. Assess, measure, and hold yourself accountable with other CEOs doing the very same work. If you will not allocate that ideal quarterly time, schedule a retreat twice a year as a minimum refresher for your software upgrading; you can never remain current without an improved process. It cannot be done.

Keep yourself current.

Keep your team current.

Adopt your own process to secure that outcome.

I have found the results so refreshing for CEOs who engage SUPER CHANGE processes for their teams. SUPER CHANGE leaders report explosive outcomes in growth and replenishment that were missing, as over-stress is now relieved within growing-again CEO-to-CEO communities. The switched-on, turned-on leaders are known by their adaptation to SUPER CHANGE, their social capital, and their process plan to refresh mental software. The entire organization is stimulated to do more, in less time, because the boss is walking the talk.

As a mentor to the top leaders alive today, I must report that it takes something truly *powerful* outside our workspace habits and routines to open our bandwidth to receive new mental agility. It must be achieved in CEO-level experiences of quality. It must be highly customized with maximum one-on-one mentor time. It is individual. It is first the vulnerability to a new age, the age of SUPER CHANGE. You must slow down to catch up. To pause and assess—hey, it is not personal. My leadership training was deficient. I benefit from growing leadership tools that I can apply to silo managers with new expertise in a rapidly changing market. While if it is not my genius, it is not my job, I delegate the task to expert horses pulling my wagon forward, outsourced or in-house. However, I alone must be the bridle master to speak the horse language to achieve the outcomes I desire in SUPER CHANGE, as only the CEO can direct. SUPER CHANGE is your job, your next job, your first job, as every current and forward super stress relaxes from that one next first choice. The priority is a SUPER CHANGE leadership process to remain current.

A leader who creates a list of quarterly challenges that we all face, and brings that changing matrix to superior mentors, resolves challenges with solutions that became visible from the process without the cost of delay.

In personal space, Landmark Forum and PSI World Seminars for graduates of Landmark (my father's latest work), are top-tier leadership process upgrades that CEO Space strongly endorses to our own client leadership. Every sixty to ninety days, download new software that fits your challenge areas, inside or outside. No one does it all. Having several processes you can rotate in and out is the most ideal program choice.

Advance social capital by building the priceless leadership asset base of ever-growing cooperative leadership communities. Find your process for doing this work. For example, if you can run your empire virtually, would downloading New Brain software five times a year work for you? Do you want less currency on your mental software or more frequent currency for your outcomes? How are you committing to get it?

Now you know that you never know what you do *not* know right now. You do not know what you do not know and you cannot see what you cannot see—invisible options and opportunities to the leader challenge the momentum. More options results in better outcomes and faster solutions. You do not know what you cannot know this instant.

Do you desire to commit to a process that allows you to know more than you know today? To secure new options and new opportunities for outcomes you will desire tomorrow? *Do you agree superior mentorship upgrades your core mental software?* What is your process to become current in an age of SUPER CHANGE that will remain with human beings for a thousand years or more? Do you agree the first and next priority must be you and your team upgrading the mental software that wins in SUPER CHANGE before further choices and decisions get made? Do you also agree that yesterday is already too late, due to the ongoing acceleration and speed of SUPER CHANGE setting in on leadership? Do you have the better, stronger, improved plan, team and resources? Why not?

All that remains in SUPER CHANGE is your decision to act on becoming and staying current.

I wish you godspeed. Your next miracle comes from SUPER CHANGE, and you are God's most favorite miracle of them all.

Success is a learned behavior. — Berny Dohrmann 1988

ACKNOWLEDGEMENTS

To my readers:

Super Change and its sequel *Digital Manners* could not be in your library without the top tier mentors to the corporate leaders you read about all the time, from Elon Musk, to Mark Cuban, to Meg Whitman at Hewlett Packard, to Jamie Diamond. I want to acknowledge the mentor of the mentors, and my own mentor, Roel Campos, former United States Securities and Exchange Commissioner and senior law partner to the planet shifters of this world at Hughes Hubbard & Reed in Washington DC and New York City.

I want to thank Tony Robbins for remaining next on Super Change (even now during challenges), and for cutting the ribbon on SUPER TEACHING as we SUPER CHANGED the University of Alabama. Changing the world only occurs with collaboration among the influencers.

I could never have written these tools of leadership development into one book without the fraternity of thought leaders from the great Dan Clark; to Jack Canfield of *Chicken Soup for the Soul*; Mark Victor Hansen; John Gray of *Men are from Mars, Women are from Venus*; the inspirations of Lisa Nichols; the great Les Brown; Sharon Lechter of *Rich Dad Poor Dad;* and Richard Tan of Success Resources.

Bob Proctor and I have labored on the SUPER CHANGE paradigm shift, Bob's latest and greatest product that takes his Matrixx event (invented at CEO Space) and makes it game changing for leaders. Thank you, Bob Proctor, for always being the light that shows what comes next and how to manifest it all.

To Phyllis Newhouse at Xtreme Solutions (the leading counter to cyber terrorism for industries worldwide), what a fortune that you would cross mentor with me. To Dr. Lei Lewis of *Woman of Wealth Magazine*, thank you for your leadership and full partnership for lady leaders.

John Gray, author of *Men are from Mars, Women are from Venus*, was mentored by my famous father—like Zig Ziglar, Napoleon Hill and Earl Nightingale—into SUPER CHANGE for relationships right down to when Mars and Venus collide.

My faculty at CEO Space is so large we can't acknowledge all 350 of you, but know you carry CEO Space leaders into the highest level of leadership development on Earth. Hugh Ballou, the not-for-profit leader and author of *Transforming Power: Stories from Transformational Leaders for Encouragement and Inspiration* (my story is in that bestseller); Dr. David Gruder, author of *The New IQ: How Integrity Intelligence Serves You, Your Relationships, and Our World*; Adam Markel, author of *Pivot: The Art and Science of Reinventing Your Career and Life*, which was released on the CEO Space stage and is today a bestseller; Maria Speth of Jaburg Wilk Attorneys at Law and my guide for decades; and the great Michael Bernard Beckwith of Agape International Spiritual Center in Beverly Hills, who is always a brother in this work at the soul level.

To my Hollywood producers framing SUPER CHANGE from *What Dreams May Come* with Barnet Bain, to Gene Kirkwood at Paramount, to Greg Reid of *Wish Man*, to Phil Goldfine, all bringing us into SUPER CHANGE through film, and all of my tribe in the arts.

My special acknowledgement to Cathy Lee Crosby and CLC Studios for keeping me on the right path, and to the team at SPORTOCO for what comes next in 5G. Dr. Rey Linares has kept me on this planet and now changes the world with SuperWater. My acknowledgement to Jim

Wilson for bringing us nanotechnology that makes coal burn clean with zero pollution, and to Tony Robbins for bringing us low cost, high quality organic beef, chicken, and fish proteins, all plant-based, and all without the pollution created by raising livestock.

To everyone who poured into me and are in my world and my CEO Space, may I include you in my tribe with my endorsement and acknowledgment of your magic in my life, now and forever.

Berny Dohrmann

Made in the USA
San Bernardino, CA
09 December 2019